Making It Work

Small Church in Action Series

Making It Work

Effective Administration in the Small Church

Douglas Alan Walrath

Valley Forge ® *Judson Press*

Making It Work: Effective Administration in the Small Church
© 1994
Judson Press, Valley Forge, PA 19482-0851

Bible quotations in this volume are from the HOLY BIBLE: *New International Version*, copyright 1973, 1978, 1984. Used by permission of Zondervan Bible Publishers; and from the Revised Standard Version of the Bible, copyright 1946, 1952, 1971, by the Division of Christian Education of the National Council of the Churches of Christ in the USA. Used by permission.

"An Artful Helper," from *New Possibilities for Small Churches*, edited by Douglas A. Walrath (New York: The Pilgrim Press, 1983), pp. 18-21. Reprinted by permission of publisher, The Pilgrim Press, Cleveland, Ohio.

Library of Congress Cataloging-in-Publication Data
Walrath, Douglas Alan, 1933-
    Making it work : effective administration in the small church / by Douglas A. Walrath.
    Douglas A. Walrath.
    p.   cm.
    ISBN 0-8170-1211-7
    1. Small churches. I. Title.
BV637.8.W53 1994
254—dc2094-21740

Printed in the U.S.A.

94 95 96 97 98 99 00 01 8 7 6 5 4 3 2 1

Table of Contents

90095

Preface

In the early 1970s, when a group of us gathered at Hartford Seminary to explore the unique character of small churches, only a few contemporary books about small churches were in print. Now, twenty years later, as I prepare to teach a seminary course on "Possibilities for Small Churches," the bibliography of resources designed for leaders of small congregations covers several pages. With so much information available, why offer another book about how to lead small churches?

The answer is simple. Though there are many fine books designed for leaders of small congregations, none of them focus on administration. The accepted wisdom seems to be that administration in small churches is either unnecessary or impossible! This book is designed to fill the void and to demonstrate that administration in small churches is both necessary and possible.

Administration in small churches is different because small churches *are* different. Administrative approaches designed for midsized and large congregations are not suited for small churches—as many frustrated administrators have discovered. Effective administration in small churches is possible only when administrators understand, accept, and honor the unique character of small churches.

In the first two chapters of this book I describe what I believe to be essential understandings, attitudes, and approaches that can enable administrators to serve faithfully and effectively with small churches. I intend that the reader take these understandings, attitudes, and approaches to heart. They *are* essential. One must accept and internalize them before trying to do administration in a small congregation. To serve people well one must first of all respect them.

Chapters 3 and 4 offer practical suggestions administrators can utilize in their ministry with small congregations. These suggestions are designed to help administrators practice administration according to the theory presented in chapters 1 and 2. Appendix I contains some tools I have found useful in my work with small congregations and those who lead them.

In Appendix II Frank Rogers-Groggett offers a critical overview of personal computer resources designed for small congregations. I asked Frank to write this appendix because his experience and wisdom in the world of the personal computer far exceeds mine. He came to Bangor Seminary in midlife after working with computers in industry for many years; he now applies that accumulated expertise as a pastor and administrator in a small congregation.

This is the fourth and last book I expect to write about ministry with small congregations. For many years most of those who sat in meetings I attended were older than I was; now most are younger. As time passes I more and more find myself drawing on the insights of others who now are setting the pace of ministry with small churches. There are many able leaders today with rich insights to share. One of the rewards of editing this series of books for leaders of small churches is the opportunity it gives me to discover new voices who describe in new ways how small churches can be faithful in these days.

At the Hartford meeting twenty years ago someone observed prophetically that "small churches are here to stay." They are. Though small churches will no doubt pass in and out of fashion, and many will struggle to survive, small churches will always be with us.

As they read the pages that follow, my friends in ministry with small churches will recognize again how much they have contributed to me. Many times when I am sure an insight is mine I discover that it really came from someone else. I try to be careful to give credit where it is due. If I have failed to mention some as sources, I hope they will recognize that the oversights are not intentional.

A few deserve special mention. C. Scott Planting, who serves as pastor of the three small congregations that form the parish where I am a member, is the most outstanding minister I have ever met of *any* size church. I marvel repeatedly at what he knows and what he does. Janet McAuley is equally gifted. Every time I watch Maine Public Television's documentary on her ministry and see her trudge through the fall leaves on a country road dressed in the garb of an Episcopal priest and a blaze orange hunter's hat, I see again why she is so effective. I know that these two who appear so outstanding to me are actually representative of many more. But in writing this book I have drawn heavily on the insights they have shared with me, and I offer them my special thanks.

Douglas Alan Walrath

Chapter 1

How to Be a Faithful and Realistic Administrator

When I told one of my friends I was writing a book about administration in small churches, he laughed. "What can you say?" he asked me.

"I hope I can offer some suggestions that are both faithful and practical," I told him. And I went on to describe how I think faithful and practical go together. Jesus, as we see him in the Gospels, is as practical as he is faithful. How else could he have convinced rural, working people to become his disciples? They could *see* that he was more than just talk. "Come with me and you will learn how to fish for people" (Mark 1:17, my translation). They went with him because they believed he could catch fish.

More than thirty years of working with leaders in small churches has convinced me that those who effectively lead small churches are as practical as they are faithful. They know what they can expect from God; they know what they can expect of themselves; and they know what they can expect from their churches. Knowing what you *can* expect and *how* to draw that out is the ministry of administration. Administration joins know-how to faith.

Administration is concerned with the *corporate* life of a congregation. Leaders who exercise the ministry of administration help their congregation set appropriate and possible goals; they tend the day-to-day life of the church so that it functions smoothly and efficiently as an organization; they guide a congregation to use their resources purposefully and faithfully. In

1

their role as administrators, leaders help a congregation to be faithful and effective as a church. In the words of St. Paul:

> To each is given the manifestation of the Spirit for the common good. . . And God has appointed in the church first apostles, second prophets, third teachers, then workers of miracles, then healers, helpers, administrators . . .(1 Corinthians 12:7, 28, RSV).

Respect: the Essential Foundation

Administration with small churches is different because small churches *are* different. Effective administrators of small churches may not be experts on administration in general, but they do understand how small churches are different. They don't assume that leaders in small churches should simply adapt approaches designed for large churches.

Anyone who wants to lead small churches effectively must respect them. Recently some colleagues who are pastors of small churches in Maine attended a "required" training event for all the clergy of their denomination in our state. The focus of the event was church growth. The leadership team were all "from away"—a term local people here often use to describe those who aren't native Mainers *and* who are not in touch with Maine life and culture. The first speaker at the workshop began by stating that the theory and methods she would share are appropriate for all kinds of churches, small as well as large. One of those present interrupted her: "Will you please distinguish large churches from small?" She responded quickly and categorically, "Large churches have about 5,000 members; small churches have about 500 members." Raucous laughter erupted in the group. "What's so funny?" the speaker asked. A member of the group explained the laughter: "Even the largest church in our denomination in this state does not have 500 members."

No doubt the workshop leader was well intentioned, but she was ill-informed. She was well prepared to talk about church growth, but not in terms suited or useful to those gathered. She reminds me of a respected and well-known national church leader who said recently that no congregation with fewer than 125 members is "viable." That may be his experience, but he is also ill-informed.

The facts contradict both of these "authorities"—both past and present facts. I began my ministry thirty-five years ago as pastor of a 120-member church, and today I belong to a 90-member church. Both of these congregations were viable thirty-five years ago and both are viable today. They are financially sound, psychologically healthy, nurturing, serving communities of faith. Their vitality would challenge many other churches both large and small. During the years I served as a denominational executive and consultant, I worked with scores of similarly viable small churches.

Nonetheless, I am well aware that the perspective reflected by the woman leading the church growth workshop resembles that of many of the most influential church leaders today. I have often asked myself why there is so much disparity between my perspective and that of so many current "authorities" in the church world. The answer may lie in our different personal experiences of church life.

I think all of our perspectives are molded much more by our individual day-to-day, firsthand experiences than most of us recognize. During the years I was a denominational executive, I attended a variety of events that brought together denominational staff, seminary teachers, and others who provide services and leadership development for small churches. At one of these events, perhaps because he found some of the descriptions of small churches unrelated to the church in which he participated, a local leader from a small church asked, "How many of you who serve as consultants to small churches actually participate personally in a small congregation? Please raise your hand, if you do." To my surprise I alone raised my hand.

Though small churches still compose the majority of American congregations, as far as many influential church leaders are concerned, small churches are not the accepted norm today. While many examples of faithful and viable small congregations exist, nearly all the congregations they hold up as models of "viable" churches are large—usually very large. A well-known church consultant captures the dominant mood in one sentence: "The future belongs to the 'mega-church.'"

This perspective shapes a majority of the books, articles, videotapes, seminary courses, and other training events that focus on church leadership. Most of these assume that pastors and other church leaders need to be equipped to lead large churches. Most of those who produce these materials and events know that a majority of congregations are and will remain small. In the foreseeable future a majority of church leaders will serve in small congregations. But the prevailing point of view implies that effective leaders will either want to move quickly beyond these "entry level" congregations or learn how to help these small congregations grow or join together to become larger. It is not surprising that contemporary leaders who find themselves in a small church often pressure the congregation to grow. They don't know how to lead a small congregation effectively. For many, a small congregation is by definition inadequate.

I understand their dilemma. Methods of ministry, including methods of administration, that are workable in one kind of church often do not transfer easily to another kind of church. In my own ministry I have experienced the frustration of trying to make approaches learned in one kind of church work in another kind. After seven years of service with that 120-member church to which I was called early in my ministry, I left to answer a call to become the senior pastor of a suburban church with nearly 1,000 members. The transition was very difficult.

Hardly anything I learned to do in my ministry with the small church worked in the large church. In short order I discovered that the pattern of visitation I had established in the small church would not work in the large church. I would *never* be able to visit all the families in the parish; most people in the new parish expected me to make an appointment, not simply drop in unannounced. My approach to sermon writing was equally unworkable in the new church. My informal method of writing my sermon throughout the week, sometimes not deciding the Scripture or title until Thursday or Friday, faltered in the face of a church bulletin that had to be ready go to the printer on Tuesday morning. I also discovered that my spontaneous, do-what-needs-to-be-done-today administrative style was equally inappropriate, as I faced a secretary prepared to keep my schedule of appointments and a co-pastor and director of religious education who needed to integrate their work and schedules with mine.

Within a week I realized that my rural, small-church patterns of ministry would not work in this large, suburban congregation. But I found it surprisingly difficult to change my ways of ministering. Though I realized the old, familiar patterns wouldn't work in the new church, I found myself again and again following them. I kept trying to function informally because I felt that I *should* be able to work informally in the large church long after I knew an informal approach didn't fit there.

I faltered in the new church because I was unprepared for the fact that large churches are not *somewhat* different from small churches, they are *radically* different. In the same radical way that a Wal-Mart is different from a corner store, so a large church is radically different from a small one.[1] We can appreciate the fundamental differences between small and large businesses and between small and large churches only when we recognize that these differences are primarily cultural. Small and large are not simply different points on quantitative scales of businesses and churches. A small church differs from a large church *in kind*, as radically as an extended family differs from a shopping center. What is appropriate and functional in one is not appropriate or workable in the other. And, as I discovered through hard experience, no matter how hard we may try, we can't make it work.

In those early years of my ministry I was unaware of how deeply our norms, personal preferences, leadership know-how and theology are defined together within a primary church culture. What we know how to do, what we believe works, what we feel comfortable doing, what we think is suitable for others, what we believe will enable others to be faithful all reflect and are reinforced by our own personal experience. We seek and find nurture and are most comfortable as leaders in a congregation that fits us. In other kinds of congregations we often feel uncomfortable; in some we feel like misfits.

Our instinctive sense of what can and should work in any congregation reflects our primary church culture. The attitudes and norms that govern us as leaders reflect that culture. The difficulties that stem from the lack of raised hands among the executives and seminary professors present at that conference are rooted in their lack of ongoing personal involvement with small churches. Those who do not seek an ongoing relationship with a small church need to use extreme caution when they define what small churches "need to become." If they can't feel for and with small churches, there is a good chance they will misjudge what those congregations can and should become. They may misguide those they advise.

It is not easy to guide appropriately those whose gifts, visions, and needs are different from our own. Years ago when my children were young and I was complaining about one of them, a friend observed that a parent's greatest challenge is to nurture a child who is different from him or her. Similarly, I think it takes an unusually sensitive and sympathetic leader to help a congregation become what he or she does not find personally meaningful, particularly if that congregation does not fit the prevailing cultural norms for congregations.

To lead a small church effectively we must be able to identify and reject suggestions that are not appropriate. When I was a denominational executive, I attended a conference on church growth at the ten-thousand-member Garden Grove Community Church in Orange County, California. What I learned proved to be very useful in my current ministry. I carried research and planning responsibilities for new church development at the time. I found the insights of the conference staff, most notably those offered by Robert Schuller, the church's senior pastor, immensely helpful in my work with new church development fields.

Some months later at a denominational meeting I was pleasantly surprised to see a pastor I had met at the Garden Grove event. At the time he was serving a small church in rural Wisconsin. He told me excitedly that he had just convinced his church board to appropriate funds to build a parking lot around his church. "Why?" I inquired. "Your church is located out at a rural crossroad; people park easily along the roadsides." Then he shared his rationale for the parking lot: He had learned at the church growth conference that churches will grow when they have an excess of parking spaces.

This leader transferred what he learned in one context uncritically to another. The widespread belief that those who lead small churches should seek to fulfill visions and apply methods appropriate for large churches is misguided. The differences between the two are profound. To imagine that one will be equipped to lead one kind of church by learning methods that are suitable for another is like imagining that a physician could be prepared to practice psychiatry by completing a residency in urology.

How to Qualify As a Leader in a Small Church

To be an effective administrator in a small church you must first be accepted as a leader by that congregation. To be affirmed by them you must appreciate and affirm that small congregation. To affirm them does not mean you accept them uncritically; it means you recognize and affirm their inherent value and potential as a church.

Most small churches are rooted in a minority culture. I am using "minority" here as a cultural term, not as an ethnic or a numerical term. Rural people and black people are both cultural minorities. Rural people are not necessarily an ethnic minority as well—unless they happen to be black or Native American or members of some other ethnic minority. But rural people, even white rural people, are a cultural minority in the United States today and within the organizational life of mainline denominations. The fact that they are rooted in a minority culture shapes the life and attitude of small congregations.

The way a particular small church functions depends on the character of the minority culture in which it is rooted. Typical small churches may reflect a rural culture, an ethnic culture, or the culture of those with an alternate lifestyle, such as gays and lesbians. The character traits that are native to a culture shape the life of small congregations rooted in that culture.

Members of small churches also tend to be emotionally and psychologically rooted in their church. Most of those who choose to participate in a small church not only want to belong to a small church, they believe they function best as members of that particular congregation. Members of small churches characteristically experience an interdependent relationship with their congregation. They belong to it; it belongs to them. Many have never been members of any other church. Many believe they wouldn't fit well, much less be able to thrive either in another culture or another church. To suggest that they could fit easily in another church feels to them like suggesting they easily could exchange their marriage partner of forty years for another.

These specific and local commitments that are typical of members of small churches contrast radically with the mobility and often tentative local commitments that are central characteristics of middle-class, majority American culture. Pastors and other church leaders who have their roots in majority culture are often baffled and sometimes even angered by attitudes exhibited by members of small churches who seem alternately provincial or stubborn to cultural outsiders.

One very urbane pastor and spouse told me they can continue year after year to serve the remote coastal area where they minister only because they periodically are able to "escape" to the city for renewal. They also accept the fact that most of the local people in their congregation don't understand their need to go away from time to time. After one particularly exciting three-day escape, the next Sunday at the coffee hour following worship the spouse described in animated terms the concerts, museums, and other stimulating events they had enjoyed in the city. When she finished, a local lobsterman who had listened courteously to her exuberant story with a puzzled look on his face responded, "I can't understand why you would want to be away when it was nice here all week."

Those who thrive locally have no need to go away. They don't want to move on or away or "up." The oft-quoted Maine native's remark to the tourist, "I never hurry," suggests that there is nothing to hurry to get to. What matters is here. Father Kenneth Lindsey, who retired a few years ago after a long ministry with small, rural Episcopal parishes, told me that his ministry had been so fruitful because he honored one central idea he learned in a rural sociology course in seminary: "You always need to remember when working with rural people that where they are is the center of the world for them." That's also true of their feelings about their church. In fact, it describes the feelings of members of most small churches about their church: the congregation where they are is the center of the church for them.

Whether a leader experiences this kind of commitment as devotion or stubbornness depends on whether the leader recognizes the potential or only the possible difficulties it represents. Initially, outsiders to a culture often see some of its central characteristics in negative terms. To appreciate a culture one must first of all try to see those who represent it positively.

One of my favorite friends is deaf. One day a well-meaning social worker, thinking it would be kind to soften the designation "deaf," referred to him as "hearing impaired." He responded strongly, "I am *not* hearing impaired; I am deaf."

If I designate my deaf friend, Curtis, as "hearing impaired," I describe him in terms of what he cannot do. I also define him negatively in relation to my world and culture, which is hearing, not positively in relation to his world and culture, which is deaf. To describe a church as "small" is similar to describing someone as "deaf." Unlike "hearing impaired" or "small membership," both "deaf" and "small" are essentially positive terms. The designation "small-membership" church, like the designation "hearing-impaired person," focuses our attention on what the church or person lacks—an adequate amount of members or hearing. Viewing small churches or deaf persons positively as small or deaf opens us to their potential. It encourages us to appreciate their unique, inherent value—to see what they have to offer, both individually and as representatives of the culture to which they belong.

To be open to the potential of a culture we have to respect those who represent it. When they "rub us the wrong way," we have to move beyond our negative feelings. We have to extend ourselves. To communicate with Curtis I have had to learn sign language. That has not been easy for me. In spite of my effort to master it, sign language still seems alien to me; I am not good at it. I am humbled by my inadequacy and am very self-conscious. Curtis can see that I am not good at sign language. I wonder at his ability to understand me. But he suffers with my fumbling effort because he knows it represents caring and respect for him.

As I learn Curtis's language I glimpse his world. It is different, the deaf world. I am beginning to discover how and why it is different. For example, some would say he and other deaf people are stubborn and suspicious. But, as I have learned about Curtis's world, I have come to realize that deaf people are often socially isolated, like small churches, and need to figure things out for themselves. And I realize that deaf people are frequently abused by the hearing majority who think they know what is good for them. I understand now why Curtis thinks for himself and is cautious with nondeaf persons.

I am even learning from Curtis to see things differently in the world we share in common. I grew up on the west side of Chicago. I am an immigrant to rural culture, as well as a newcomer to the world of the deaf. I am still learning about the rural world where I now live.

Curtis is a native, rural Mainer, as well as deaf. Like many deaf people, he sees more carefully than many hearing people.

As we walked through my garden the other afternoon I pulled up a "weed" and threw it on the ground. Curtis picked it up, took a bite of it, and handed it back to me. "That's wild lettuce," he signed. "You can eat it." And for the next few minutes I learned that many of the plants I have been pulling up and discarding as "weeds" are actually good for food.

Like my deaf friend, a small church represents a rich world. A leader "from away" can learn about that potential only from those who belong—insiders who know the culture the church reflects. In the process of becoming acquainted, a leader is likely to discover that some people who initially seem to be "weeds" are really sources of nurture. When Sherry, my wife, and I first began to participate in our local church, one woman seemed particularly difficult to us. One day we complained openly about her ways to our pastor. "Give her time," he said. "You will grow to appreciate her." We have. We see now what she gives and rarely notice what at first made her seem so difficult.

To become a qualified leader in a small church you must first affirm that congregation and be willing to be led by them—even the difficult ones.

Small Churches Have Hidden Potential

To lead a small church faithfully and effectively we need to be able to see into that church. We have to appreciate its essential character. Before I describe how we can see into a small church, I think it is important to distinguish between churches that are only temporarily small and those that are likely to remain small. Most of the churches I call "small" or "smaller" will always be limited in size; those that are only temporarily small I call "not-yet-big" churches. The suggestions in this book are intended primarily for leaders in churches that are likely to remain small.

Not-yet-big churches are only temporarily small. For this reason leaders in not-yet-big churches will find that many of the suggestions I offer in this book do not apply to them. During my years as a church development consultant, I worked with many not-yet-big churches. The purpose of my work with them was to help them grow, not to help them become effective small churches. I knew that if they became effective small churches, they probably would not grow.

Most not-yet-big churches are either new church starts or one of those unusual small churches that has both the opportunity and capability to become a midsized or larger church. From their very beginnings new church starts are constituted and should be viewed as churches that are only temporarily small. Leaders in this kind of church need to avoid strengthening the relational, single-focus, extended-family style of congregational life that is essential in other kinds of small churches. Encouraging a close-knit pattern of relationships among the members of a not-yet-big church may impede its growth into the diverse, program-focused congregation it is designed to become. Presenting a not-yet-big church as a small church to its community is misleading and dysfunctional. It encourages people to join who want and need a small church. When the church becomes large, it can no longer meet their needs or fit their capabilities.

The two kinds of small churches I have in view as I write this book are the stable small church and the smaller church. When I use the term "small church," these are the kinds of congregations I picture. By their very nature they are likely to remain small; their limited size makes them accessible and nurturing to those they serve. True small churches can become more faithful and effective, but not by becoming larger. When their membership increases they become inaccessible and unable to nurture those who thrive best in a small congregation.

The stable small church has usually been small for some time. It continues year after year with only slight fluctuations in size because its leaders either consciously or unconsciously know how to maintain it as it is. They may not know how to help it be more effective or faithful, but they do know how to help it persist.

When I was about to begin my work as a synod executive, I remember riding along a tollway with my predecessor. As we passed one of the small churches for which I would be responsible, he said, "That's the ____ Church. They have only about forty active members. And hardly any of them are capable of having children. The average member is probably seventy years old. I don't see how they will survive more than another ten years." Twenty years later, several years after I had left that position, I happened to be riding on the same road with my successor. We passed the same church, and he uttered almost exactly the same words! "That's the ____ Church . . . . The average member is probably seventy years old. I don't see how they will survive more than another ten years."

"I wouldn't worry about them," I responded. "Casey expressed exactly the same concern when he was orienting me nearly twenty years ago. At first I was worried about them. But every time I visited during the twelve years I was synod executive they always seemed to have about the same number of members. Finally I figured out how they survive. It's not some miraculous lack of aging. It's true that most of them are too old to have kids. But as members die, more retirees move into the area and take their places. For years they have maintained their membership by replacing those who die with younger members in their sixties."

Stable small churches know how to persevere. One needs only to watch them for awhile to discover the secret of their persistence. It usually resides in the fact that they accept their smallness and have learned how to live within the resources they have.

Those who do not accept or understand small churches often view them categorically as lethargic—and some of them are. Unperceptive administrators who try to push small churches to grow according to preconceived plans usually discover that the imposed programs are alien and even beyond the capability of the church's members. Most of the time it is a mistake to interpret their resistance to change as simple stubbornness. It almost always represents a legitimate refusal to change in ways that they sense are not good for them.

Leaders who are open and willing to learn how a small church can become more faithful *as a small church* often discover that the energetic stubbornness that enables the church to survive can be redirected. Members of a small church in Albany, New York, composed (like the congregation near the tollway) almost entirely by retirees, refused to follow the prescribed patterns for the revitalization of city neighborhood churches. Year after year their church declined. Then a new pastor encouraged them to redirect their determination to survive. He spoke directly to the older persons who composed the majority of the church's members. In effect he said, "If you want to keep your church, I think you are going to have to reach out. Otherwise it will die when you die." Then he said, "You have talent, you have experience, and you have time to give in Christian service." The corps of senior citizens rose to the challenge! The congregation now offers a wide range of ministries: from helping to furnish nourishing meals to senior citizens who live alone, to providing neighborhood residents with information they need to gain access to social services to which they are entitled. New senior citizens are now attracted to the church to join its ministries. What outsiders to a congregation may see only as stubbornness often represents energy that can propel a small church into a vital future.

Helping smaller churches become more faithful is often more difficult than helping stable small churches. Most smaller churches live in the shadow of their past—the overwhelming memory of better days. Members may be so obsessed with the need to recover what they used to be, that they can't consider any other options. If someone suggests how they might move ahead, they respond by describing what they need to get back to.

When I proposed to the leaders of one city neighborhood smaller church composed entirely of members over fifty years of age that they begin ministries to new residents of their area by sharing their church building with a new Spanish-speaking congregation, they were obviously not interested. When I asked what they would suggest instead, they responded in one voice, "We need to rebuild our Sunday school the way it used to be. Then we will have a source of new members and be on the road back to the church we once were."

"But," I said, "there are hardly any English-speaking children in your neighborhood."

"Then we will draw them in from the suburbs," one of them countered. He then went on to describe the dramatic growth of a suburban church ten miles away, as if they could draw new members from the area it serves. Only after they had tried one more time and failed again to move ahead by turning the clock back, were they willing to join forces with a congregation a block away and together seek a viable future. So long as it is dominated by memories, a smaller church cannot move ahead.

A small church's unique character, shaped by its own particular history and circumstances, determines its potential. We gain the most useful and realistic estimate of the potential of a small church when we are in touch with its character. In this book I will describe a variety of frames of reference I have found useful for administrators who want to identify and guide small congregations to develop their potential. Each of these frames of reference can be a window that helps leaders to describe the unique character of a small church. I rarely use a frame of reference as a source of categories in which to place small churches. I have found that categorizing small churches often hides more than it reveals.

In his helpful book *Transforming a People of God*, Denham Grierson suggests that categorizing congregations actually leads us away from rather than toward the insights we need to gain to unlock the potential of our own church.[2] When we think of a church within a category to which we assign it, we then perceive the church *in terms of the characteristics of the category* rather than in terms of itself. For example, suppose we use "rural" as a category and "reluctant to change" as a behavior associated with that category. Following the logic of categorization, once we categorize a church as "rural," we assume it is reluctant to change.

Grierson proposes an entirely different approach, which I find much more fruitful when working with small churches. He suggests that we utilize analytical schemes as frames of reference to help us identify the key characteristics of individual congregations, rather than as sources of categories in which to place them. Each frame of reference becomes a tool that helps us picture how a particular congregation functions. Rather than classifying a church as "small" and then assuming the congregation will behave according to a preconceived description of small churches, Grierson suggests that we look through the frame of reference "small" to identify how *this* congregation functions. Each frame of reference becomes a window that helps us see more fully what a congregation is and what it might become.

I find Grierson's approach particularly well suited to small congregations. Often we can identify a small congregation's potential only if we can grasp their uniqueness. Several years ago a new minister tried to work with a very small congregation not far from where I live. In a few days he was sure about what they were like (rural) and certain of both how they needed to change (reach out to their community) and what prevented them from changing ("just plain stubborn"). In a matter of weeks he was alienated from them; in only a few months he left. "They will never amount to anything," he told me angrily. "They don't even deserve to be called a church."

This past fall one of the residents in the Small Church Leadership Program at Bangor Seminary, where I teach, was assigned to the same congregation. Susan had never worked in a rural area before, but she is a single parent, wise beyond her years, patient, and full of faith. In the classroom during a previous term, she and other residents worked their way through Grierson's frames of reference, learning how to use each as a window to get in touch with the character of the congregations in which they were beginning to serve. As Susan began her ministry with the congregation that had so frustrated the previous pastor, she brought no preconceived images or expectations. She let them impress her.

For the first few weeks Susan was baffled and sometimes discouraged. Then one afternoon she was meeting with a few women for Bible study and prayer. They began to talk to her about their struggles: living with abusive husbands and being left alone to run a household and raise children. Susan was moved by the suffering and courage represented in the group. She encouraged them to design a series of gatherings that would be helpful to women like them. With her encouragement they did. At one meeting a woman who is a therapist helped those who gathered to build self-esteem; at another meeting a woman who is a carpenter helped them learn how to make simple home repairs. At the last meeting Susan glimpsed the potential in their persistence. Several women said, "I think we should do this again."

This student minister discovered where to begin to help her smaller congregation grow in faith by seeing and accepting their uniqueness as a very small church composed entirely of women. As we talked one day about her church, I couldn't help but recall the pastor who left angrily because the members were "not committed." "I can't be angry that they give so little," Susan said. "With the burdens they carry mostly by themselves, I marvel that they have anything at all left to give."

If we who serve as administrators in small churches want our congregations to grow in faith and become more effective, we must define our approach according to the character of our congregation. We must discern and respect the way God is already at work in our congregation. When residents in the small-church program at Bangor Seminary are ready to begin

ministry with a congregation, I always send them off with a
theological suggestion. "Remember that you do not have to take
God to your congregation; God is already there. When you begin
to see how God is at work in them, you will begin to know how
to minister with them."

Questions for Reflection and Discussion

1. What kinds of small church(es) do you serve? Describe the
   unique character of the congregation(s) you lead.

2. For each congregation, make a list of strong points and
   another list of characteristics that concern you and may need
   attention.

3. How well do your own sympathies, values, and beliefs match
   the size, culture, and capabilities of the congregation(s)? In
   what respects do your natural inclinations and prejudices
   match those of the congregation(s)?

4. Ask yourself and others to describe occasions during the past
   few years that illustrate how God is present and working in
   the congregation(s).

Notes

1. The standard work on corporate culture is Terence E. Deal
and Allen A. Kennedy, *Corporate Cultures: The Rites and Rituals
of Corporate Life* (Reading, Mass.: Addison-Wesley Publishing
Company, Inc., 1982). The basic text that describes the different
dynamics of small and large settings is Allan W. Wicker, *An
Introduction to Ecological Psychology* (Monterey, Calif.:
Brooks/Cole Publishing Company, 1979).

2. Denham Grierson, *Transforming a People of God* (Melbourne,
Australia: The Joint Board of Christian Education of Australia and
New Zealand, 1984). Available in the United States from More-
house-Barlow.

Chapter 2

How to Be a Relational Administrator

One day this past spring, after a particularly heavy rain, the water stopped coming out of the faucets in our old farmhouse. That happens every spring; sometimes it stops flowing three or four times during March and April. Our water comes from a reservoir built one hundred years ago halfway up the hill behind the house. The reservoir captures the water that flows constantly from a spring, even during times of drought. Local people, whose families have lived here for generations, say the spring has never failed. I know that it has not run dry in the twelve years we have owned the farm.

I call the seminary to let them know I will be an hour late. They understand; they have grown accustomed to this professor who is half farmer. I put on my snowshoes and climb the hill. When I arrive at the reservoir I reach into the water and raise the end of the plastic pipe that runs to the house. Sure enough the strainer is clogged. I clean it with the old brush that I leave hanging on a tree nearby for this purpose. I am careful to keep the strainer under the water so the system doesn't lose its prime. I work quickly; the water is about forty-five degrees.

By the time I have climbed back down the hill, the water has begun to flow again from the faucets. I clean up and exchange my farmer clothes for my professor clothes. I turn on the kitchen faucet and watch the stream coming out of it. I can tell by the way it flows that everything will be back to normal by the time I return from teaching.

When I arrive at the seminary, a colleague who has heard about the water problem asks, "Don't you ever wish you could just call a plumber?"

"No," I respond, "I really don't." He looks puzzled by my response; but he has a class to teach and no time to wait for me to explain.

Fits and Misfits

There was a time when I didn't understand why the way I function puzzles some people. That was before I recognized how deeply the idea that plumbers ought only to do plumbing and professors ought only to teach is etched into contemporary American culture. One popular adage captures the dominant assumption: "You wouldn't want a plumber to take out your appendix, would you?"

I have never fit neatly into a narrow role; I always keep stepping over the cultural boundaries prescribed for ministers and professors. Some members of my church board bluntly told me I should keep to my minister role soon after I moved from the small, rural church to become the senior minister in the large suburban church. The sexton was out of town one day when the sink in the church kitchen became clogged. Several applications of chemical drain openers failed to open it. The women's circle preparing food were quite concerned. A large group would soon arrive for a luncheon. "Probably it's full of grease," I said. "I can get it open." I ignored their surprised looks and went home, took a crescent wrench out of my toolbox, returned and opened the grease trap. I cleaned it out and put it back together. The whole operation took no more than thirty minutes. I washed up and went back to work in my office.

I think the news that the pastor fixes drains created more of a stir than even the radical theological statements I sometimes made when I was serving that church. But I was the one most surprised when I heard that my successful repair did not seem praiseworthy in the eyes of some members of my church board. That I would interrupt "my work" to unstop a drain seemed inappropriate to them. "Next time, call a plumber," was their clear message to me. Unstopping drains was not included in my job description.

I recognize now that I became a "character" in their eyes when I put on overalls and fixed a drain—and not an appealing character. My plumbing seemed unprofessional, unbefitting for the senior minister of this large church. It evidently made some of them wonder whether I was suited for the position. Years later I can look back and understand why they were concerned. I did not do well as a senior minister because most of the time I would rather fix a drain than preside at a staff meeting.

I am similarly viewed as a "character" by some of those at the seminary where I teach, as well as by some researchers and professors who are my professional colleagues. Though I have worked long enough at the seminary for people there to get used to me, my "unprofessional" behavior doesn't surprise most of them anymore. They can see how it fits with, and fits me for, the kind of teaching I do: helping new ministers learn how to be effective leaders in small congregations.

The same kinds of behavior that seem odd in one context don't seem at all odd in another. What is surprising and out of place in one world seems a matter of course in another. While my colleagues in the large church and professional world are surprised that I fix my own plumbing, my rural neighbors assume that I should be able to fix it. The fact that I do my own repairs doesn't impress them because they do the same. As a matter of fact, they look down their noses at clergy and other professionals who can't make simple repairs to faucets and drains.

Different kinds of contexts support and require different kinds of leaders. There are valid reasons that govern what those in different contexts admire and criticize in their leaders. Leaders prove their worth in different ways in different contexts because being an effective leader in each context requires different attitudes, different approaches, and different skills. The old farmer who criticized the skills of recent graduates of most seminaries with the sharp comment, "The trouble with ministers today is that they're overeducated and undertrained; they know a lot but they can't do anything!" was largely accurate within the context of the rural culture out of which he spoke. But then so were the leaders in that large, suburban church when they criticized my style of leadership there. Being a senior minister who carries responsibility for administration in a large church requires the temperament and skill of an executive. I have neither. What is more, I don't want to develop them. I know my gifts and where I can use them; I know where I fit and where I am a misfit. Each of us is effective and can sustain faithful ministry in some places and not in others. Effective administrators celebrate their gifts and accept their limitations. They know where they fit.

Relational Administration

Before an administrator can discover *what to do* in a small church, he or she must become comfortable and know *how to function* within the unique dynamics that are characteristic of small churches. In this chapter I will concentrate on how faithful administrators *function* effectively in small churches. In the chapters that follow I will focus on what administrators *can do* to help small churches be faithful and effective.

In chapter 1 I described small churches as inherently local and relational institutions. Their past experience with "outsiders" makes members of many small churches suspicious of administrators who function "professionally" and organizationally. Their first concern is not whether an administrator is efficient or effective, but whether he or she is devoted to them. They trust the leader who belongs, or who clearly wants to be in a committed relationship with them. An administrator with minimal skills who belongs in a small congregation will fare far better than one who is highly skilled but detached. Members of small churches will respond with both energy and faith to the devoted ministry of a relational administrator.

I first understood the nature of relational administration some years ago when I asked a tree surgeon named Mr. Churchill to care for one of my trees. It was a pivotal experience for me and I often recall it.[1] I called Mr. Churchill because one of my trees, a tall basswood, had leafed out poorly for two summers, especially at the top. I talked about the tree with a friend who was more familiar with the locale than I, inquiring about someone who might be able to help. He said he knew of only two persons who did that kind of work: one was a botanist who was associated with the science department at a nearby university and the other was Mr. Churchill, who lived in a small village in the opposite direction. So far as my friend knew, the botanist was competent—and expensive. Mr. Churchill was not as expensive but was a character. Even so, many people preferred him.

I first called the botanist, and he arrived late in the afternoon for a "consultation" on his way home from the university. He gazed solemnly at the tree. Yes, it was diseased, obviously the result of an infestation of insects that carried the disease into the top of the tree where the leaves were stunted and falling off. There was hope, however; the tree could be saved. He knew of one chemical that would kill the bugs and another that would arrest the progress of the disease, but it would take several treatments. The cost would be about one hundred dollars per treatment, or about four hundred dollars in all, depending on how the tree responded. He would guarantee nothing and said he should start the treatments without delay.

He was annoyed when I told him I wanted to obtain a second opinion, and most especially when I mentioned this opinion was to be offered by Mr. Churchill. But I persisted.

Churchill arrived at 8:30 the next morning. He appeared to be in his late fifties, weather-beaten but still strong. "Churchill's my name," he said, as he gripped my hand. "This the tree?" I nodded. "Well, let's have a look." He stood there for a time and pondered the tree. Then he looked at me with searching eyes and asked a question for which I was totally unprepared: "Do you love your tree?"

"Why . . . of course!" I stammered, the overstatement obviously an attempt to compensate for my hesitancy.

"Then I'll see what I can do." He walked back to his truck and returned with a pair of binoculars. He looked at the tree from various angles. "Just as I suspected," he said. "You can't tell much about a tree from a distance." Again he walked back to his truck and this time returned with a set of climbing spurs attached to his heavy boots. He proceeded to climb the massive tree, all the way up into the thin-leafed top, higher than the roof of my Victorian house. I scrambled about to avoid the pieces of dead wood that tumbled down as he climbed upward.

Soon he was back on the ground. "Well, the tree's got problems," he said. "When did the lightning strike it?" I replied that I had not known lightning struck it. "Well, it did," he went on, "and a damn good thing the tree was there, because if it hadn't been, that lightening would have hit your house and probably burned it to the ground. Your tree's done you more good than you realize.

"Anyway, the tree's had a big wound ever since then and the life's been running out of it. The leaves are stunted because the good strength they need is running out of the wound. I can dress the wound, and then when the tree heals, the good strength will get back to the upper branches. Of course, we'll need to take out a few branches. A weakened tree can't support all that overgrowth; it doesn't really need it anyway."

"What about the bugs?" I asked, pointing to several crawling out of the dead wood. "Don't you have to get rid of the bugs?"

"That scientist from the university's been here, hasn't he?" he asked. I confessed that he had. "Well, he's a smart fellow, I suppose; we just don't agree on much. Them scientists work mostly with bugs in bottles. Hell, killing bugs in bottles is no trick. The trick is to kill the bugs without hurting the tree and to kill the bad bugs and not the good bugs. I'll sweep the bugs out of the wound and then dress it to keep them out. When the tree gets stronger the bugs won't bother it anymore. And you won't have all the sick birds around that you'd have if somebody started feeding the bugs chemicals. Once you start spreading those chemicals around you lose control of where they'll go."

I was becoming convinced. "Do you need to do anything more with the tree?" I asked.

"Like I said, dress the wound and prune away the dead branches. Then we need to feed it some fertilizer. You can't expect a tree to heal itself if you don't feed it."

"When can you do the work and how much will it cost me?" I asked.

He could tell I was a bit nervous. He looked at the old house and then back at me. "You make much money?" he inquired.

"No," I replied. "I'm a minister."

"Then it'll cost you ninety dollars. Can you afford ninety dollars?"

"Yes."

"You got ninety dollars right now?"

"Yes, I do."

"Well, then I can do the work right now." Which he did.

Mr. Churchill had a boy with him who was about fourteen years old and whom he introduced simply as Charlie. For the next two hours he and Charlie kept a feverish pace, he in the tree and Charlie dodging falling branches (and once the chain saw Mr. Churchill accidentally dropped from the top of the tree) and attaching tools and supplies to ropes to be hauled up into the tree. Finally, Churchill walked around the tree drilling holes a foot deep with a heavy bar. Charlie followed close behind filling each hole with fertilizer. They finished before lunchtime and I paid Mr. Churchill ninety dollars. I never saw him again. The tree recovered quite nicely just like he said it would. The bugs, by the way, gave up.

Characteristics of Relational Administrators

In my session with Mr. Churchill I discovered three essential characteristics relational administrators possess, though it took several years for me to appreciate them fully.

1. **Relational administrators honor the customs and work within the lifeways of a local culture.** Sometimes this essential respect requires the leader to adapt his or her ways of leading to function within local norms and customs. In 1978 Dr. Alan Davidson, a psychiatrist, decided to give up his suburban Toronto practice to begin a practice in rural Bracebridge, Ontario. Dr. Davidson quickly discovered that the way he practiced psychiatry in suburban Toronto would not transfer to Bracebridge. Initially he rented an office in the center of the village expecting to schedule consultations there, but no one would come to the office to see him. Psychological illness carries such a strong stigma in this rural culture that residents are unwilling to be seen visiting a psychiatrist. Davidson recognized that he would have to modify his approach to counseling to accommodate the local norms. Instead of expecting patients to come to him, he would have to go to them.

Davidson bought a four-wheel-drive vehicle and took his practice on the road. Patients still call his office to make appointments, but they don't see him there. A secretary keeps his schedule and fits clients into an itinerary for the day. On a typical day Davidson may counsel a distraught mother at her kitchen table and then meet an anxiety-ridden truck driver at a secluded spot on a dirt road. Davidson also discovered that sometimes he has to perform simple household tasks, such as helping a woman who lives alone bring in her week's supply of wood, before patients can concentrate on therapy. And Davidson learned that everyone removes their shoes before entering a rural house.

The accommodations that Davidson believes are required to practice effective therapy in this rural culture have not found wide support among his colleagues—quite the opposite. He has been labeled "unorthodox" and occasionally even been rebuked by therapists in the metropolitan-dominated medical association that oversees area physicians. But rural patients who have never consulted a psychiatrist in the past, and who say they could not go through the routine required to visit the typical psychiatrist's office, are able to consult Dr. Davidson and respond well to his rural approach to psychiatric treatment.[2]

Alan Davidson's approach to psychiatry reminds me of my friend, Janet McAuley's, approach to church administration. The fruits of her ministry with St. Martin's Episcopal Church in Palmyra, Maine, are so noteworthy that they caught the attention of a public television producer and became the subject of a documentary produced by Maine Public Broadcasting. The videotape opens with pictures of Janet walking along a rural road garbed in the traditional black shirt and clerical collar, but with a blaze orange hunting cap on her head! Both her unusual hat and the first words she speaks reveal her deep awareness of the struggles of those among whom she ministers. She describes the contest life represents in rural Maine, "Life here is hard. Most of it is spent getting ready for winter and getting through it."[3]

Janet's knowledge of the context in which she serves is hard won. A parishioner described her difficult beginnings. "Hardly anyone liked her during those first years. In fact, for the first five years of her ministry nothing much happened." But Janet refused to be put off. This former college professor (she never uses the "Dr." to which her earned degree entitles her) who prepared for ministry in her fifties, registered as a continuing education student for all the courses nearby Bangor Seminary offers in rural culture and ministry with small churches because, "My seminary had no courses that prepared me for ministry in a small parish." She noted what people criticized about her methods of ministry and modified them to fit within the local culture. Slowly local people recognized that she understood them and that she intended to challenge them to minister as a congregation to the area they serve.

With Janet's encouragement the congregation purchased and renovated a former Grange hall next to the church building. This additional building serves as a parish house for the church and as a place to house the ministries St. Martin's now offers to the entire township of Palmyra. St. Martin's has responded in exciting ways to the challenging relational administration of their devoted priest. The congregation spearheaded the development of a literacy program for adults in its area (one in four adults who live there is functionally illiterate), and a head-start program for children. They collected several thousand books and remodeled the second floor of the parish house to serve as a town library. With Janet's encouragement St. Martin's has become a food distribution center. Each year area potato farmers bring hundreds of pounds of "off-grades," misshapen but still nourishing potatoes, to the parish house and sell them at very reasonable prices or donate them to area residents with limited incomes.

When I asked her the secret of her effectiveness as an administrator in this small congregation, Janet responded, "My job is simply to help them be the church where they are." Janet's ability to guide the people of St. Martin's into ministry rests on her understanding of the nature of relational administration and her willingness to shape her leadership style to work within the local culture. The congregation took Janet seriously as a leader when they became confident of her respect and commitment to them. One parishioner summarized their decision in a crisp sentence: "When we realized she really cares about us and wouldn't go away, we decided to work with her."

2. **Relational administrators accept the potential of the congregation they serve.** They not only adapt their leadership style to suit the local context, they learn how to develop their church *from the potential represented in that congregation.* They look within, not outside, to see the church's potential. They recognize, as my pastor and friend, Scott Planting, puts it, that for better or worse "the church is who's there."

As we sat drinking coffee one day in his office at the New York State Council of Churches, Art Tennies, a colleague with whom I worked during my years as a denominational executive, expressed our mutual frustration with the day's meetings: "For years I've heard denominational leaders tell small churches they are unable. The tragedy now is that many leaders in small churches believe it." This low self-esteem is as unwarranted as it is tragic. After more than three decades of ministry with small congregations in a variety of roles—as a member, a denominational executive, a strategy consultant, and a seminary professor—I am still able to say that I have *never* found a small church that was truly "unable" *when measured by standards based on its own potential.* When I am trying to estimate the potential of a small church, I often recall the motto engraved in stone over the doorway of what was once the administration building at the former teachers' college in Albany, New York. It reads: "Let each one become all that he [or she] is able to become." With

only a slight modification that motto becomes as appropriate
for administrators who work with small churches as it is for
those who teach children: "Let each congregation become all
that they are able to become."

In either version the motto conveys a critical message to all
those who set goals for others. Standards challenge *when they
match the potential* of the person or group for whom they are
set. Challenging a person or group to meet standards that are
beyond their capability can be harmful. During my early years
as a minister, when I thought I should "progress" to become the
pastor of larger and larger congregations, I did not accept or
develop my natural ability to minister with small congregations. Instead, I struggled to become someone I am not gifted to
become. The end result of my efforts to achieve norms that do
not suit me was an emotional collapse. Years later my cousin
Howard gave me a sentence that describes my foolhardy struggle: "It's not what you eat that makes you sick, but what you
think you have to swallow!"

Jesus inspired his disciples to become faithful servants
within their own human capacities, that is, by developing their
own unique gifts and potential. Relational administrators accept their congregation's potential and help them to "become all
that *they* are able to become." Relational administrators don't
impose alien standards, especially not standards drawn from
contexts or based on kinds or sizes of churches that represent
inappropriate models. Relational administrators look first to
the congregation, not to themselves or others, to define a
church's potential.

Recently Loren Mead completed a book called *More Than
Numbers: The Ways Churches Grow.* I think Mead's work is the
most helpful and theologically appropriate description of
church growth I have ever read. He identifies four kinds of
church growth: numerical, maturational, organic and incarnational. *Numerical* growth affirms the evangelical view that a
congregation that is spiritually vital and that has the potential
in its community will challenge others to become believers.
Maturational growth represents

> the ability of a congregation to challenge, support, and
> encourage each one of its members to grow in the maturity
> of their faith, to deepen their spiritual roots, and to
> broaden their religious imagination.[4] . . .

Organic growth is about the task of building the community, fashioning the organizational structures, developing the practices and processes that result in a dependable, stable network of human relationships in which we can grow and from which we can make a difference.[5] . . .

A fourth kind of growth, *incarnational* growth, represents the "outputs" of a congregation—what

a congregation seeks to export from its life back into the life of the world, the social environment in which it exists. [Incarnational growth is] an enfleshment of the principles and faith of the congregation in the structures of the community.[6]

Mead argues that each kind of growth is an appropriate option only for congregations whose context and composition suit them for that kind. He describes how leaders can identify which kinds of growth are valid options for their church. He does not suggest that congregations can grow in only one of the four ways he identifies, nor does he believe that every congregation should be expected to grow in all four ways. He offers methods congregations can follow to identify how their own resources and opportunities equip them to grow. He puts to rest (hopefully for good) the theologically unsound notion that all congregations who live faithfully will grow numerically. I believe Mead's book should be required reading for all church leaders who are responsible to help congregations identify appropriate visions for themselves.

Discovering they are free to develop according to their own potential rather than according to imposed standards can be immensely enabling for a congregation. Several years ago I was invited to conduct a strategy consultation with a smaller congregation on Long Island, New York, that had lost members steadily for many years. The area governing body responsible to oversee the congregation was obviously frustrated by the attitudes of this "difficult" church. At the time of my visit only about forty active members remained, most of them over sixty years of age. Interest and then capital withdrawals from a modest legacy that had enabled the forty-member church to continue would last only about two more years. Their formerly Protestant, working-class neighborhood was now populated largely with Roman Catholics, most of them Spanish-speaking immigrants to the United States. This congregation was the smallest of several Protestant churches that remained in the area. All had prospered during the pre- and post-World War II years when the area developed, and then had declined as the neighborhood changed.

On a cold winter day I walked through the equally cold church building, guided by an elder whose eyes sparkled with happy memories, and sometimes with tears, as he identified people and events represented in the pictures that dotted the walls of the parish house. The feelings that came over me as he talked were surprisingly familiar. When he left and I was alone, it took only a few moments for me to recall when I had felt those feelings before. The first time was as a young pastor when I recognized I needed to tell an older parishioner, Mrs. Thompson, that I thought it was no longer safe for her to continue to live in the old Victorian house that had been her home for sixty years. There had been too many dangerous incidents—the last one only the day before when she had put on a kettle of water and become distracted; it had boiled dry and set fire to the kitchen curtains. She understood my message. For some time she had been expecting someone to bring it.

Twenty-five years later as a "strategy consultant" I found myself called to bring similar unwelcome news to the leaders of this smaller congregation. Like Mrs. Thompson, they were frightened by the prospect of leaving their home of many years. What would happened to them? Who would guide them? As a pastor I supported Mrs. Thompson as she disposed of all but the few prized possessions she could take with her when she moved out of her old homestead and into what they called in those days a "rest home." I visited her frequently during the months that followed her move. Often I marveled at the strength of character and the faith this frail woman exhibited.

Recalling what had enabled Mrs. Thompson, I suggested to leaders of the Long Island congregation that they seek a part-time pastor with relational administrative skills to guide and support them during their similarly difficult transition. They invited a retired minister to serve for one year as their transition pastor. He had the administrative knowledge and sensitivity required to lead them in this difficult time. He helped this small congregation grow in faith (Mead's maturational growth) in the process of dissolving.

They decided to offer their building for a modest sum to a new Spanish-speaking congregation. Before the old church dissolved, the pastor helped each member find a church home in another congregation. He convinced the regional jurisdiction to distribute some of the funds from legacies that would revert to the denomination when the congregation dissolved to several churches that members of the dissolving congregation planned to join. This smaller church dissolved, but it did not die. It continued to live as members took its resources to strengthen the congregations they joined. The ministry of this relational administrator helped them see and develop their unique potential. This congregation grew in faith even as it died. Like Mrs. Thompson, they became an inspiration to others.

Relational administrators identify the potential in those who compose their congregations first and then envision the ministries of their congregation. They discover how members of a congregation are gifted and then develop programs and organizational structures that fit their gifts (Mead's organic growth). The potential of small congregations like St. Martin's and smaller congregations like the forty-member church on Long Island blossom when administrators look within and help a congregation become what *they* are able to become.

3. **Relational administrators persist**. Three years ago Sherry and I produced a videotape to serve as a resource to a consultation for leaders of small churches in the United States, Canada, and the United Kingdom. The videotape traces the development of the outreach ministries of Mission-at-the-Eastward, our parish.[7] During the discussion period that followed the first showing at the consultation, one of those present asked Scott Planting, who serves as the administrative coordinator of this twelve-church parish, what enabled him to facilitate so many creative ministries. He answered simply, "I stayed. It took years before people trusted me enough to take risks with me."

There is a direct relationship between persistence and effectiveness with small churches. Several years ago at a conference, nationally known church-strategy consultant Lyle Schaller told me that his observation of pastors suggests that the most effective years of a pastor's ministry with a congregation are often the sixth, seventh, and eighth years, and then the eleventh, twelfth, and thirteenth years. Schaller's general observation applies especially to small churches. Those who

understand the realities of administration in small congregations recognize that they will not be able to introduce and
establish significant changes until they have persisted five
years or more.

Persistence is especially important when members of a small
congregation feel their survival is threatened. When small
congregations question whether they will survive, they guard
their resources with passion. To facilitate any change or
development in congregations who feel precarious requires
sensitivity and persistence. Before they are free to consider
any options, church members need to know that the leader
who asks them to take risks will be with them to face the
consequences of those risks.

Persistence is also essential when an administrator works
with a congregation that has been misguided. Small churches
that have been misled are likely to be exceptionally cautious.
Several years ago a friend who had many years of experience
guiding small churches responded to the call of a congregation
whose previous pastor left in anger. My friend spent nearly a
year becoming acquainted with the congregation and building
solid relationships with local leaders. He then proceeded slowly
and caringly to introduce what seemed to him to be appropriate
changes. Despite his careful introduction of new ideas, the
congregation resisted everything he suggested. "I didn't realize
what was wrong," he told me, "until I shifted my attention from
what they were resisting to the fact that they were resisting."
He then began to look for the source of their resistance. He
discovered it was a reaction against the way the previous pastor
had imposed changes on them, some of which were unwarranted and inappropriate.

The previous pastor was not a relational administrator. He
came to this small church with a preconceived notion of what
the congregation needed to become and imposed his ideas on
them. When they balked at his suggestions, he pressed them
even harder to implement the vision he brought to them. He
knew this church was located in an area of high poverty; he was
determined to equip the congregation to serve the needs of those
around them. Within a few months of his arrival he urged them
to develop a day-care center especially to enable single parents
of young children in the area to work.

When he submitted an application for the license required to operate the center, the pastor discovered that the two-hundred-year-old building that serves as the church's parish house would require extensive renovations to qualify. The stairways were too narrow and made of wood; the bathrooms were too small; the exterior doors opened in instead of out. He asked a local drafts-man to prepare plans showing the required changes and sub-mitted an application to a denominational agency for funds to support the remodeling. When the application was approved, members of the church board looked at the proposal seriously for the first time. They were horrified. The back stairway would be torn out and replaced by metal stairs that would come down into the church kitchen. The old wooden doors with their hand-made latches would be replaced by metal doors with "panic bar" latches. They balked at the proposal. The minister told them angrily that they were not behaving "like Christians" if they let their aesthetic concerns impede the changes needed to begin the new ministry. Under pressure they capitulated.

To qualify for federal funding the pastor also facilitated the development of an independent corporation and board to over-see the day-care center. Initial disagreements between the church board and day-care board about philosophy and budget grew more intense during the two years the day-care program operated. At the end of the second year the day-care board decided to move their program to another facility. They and the pastor left within months of each other.

When my friend learned the details of their experience with change, he understood why leaders in this small church resisted almost everything he suggested. He backed off and slowed down. He looked carefully for an area of mutual concern where the congregation could gain some positive experience with change. He discovered that he and they felt the same need to improve the church's education program. The Sunday school had faltered during the previous pastor's tenure. Over a period of several months he worked with education leaders to identify the core values they wanted to affirm in their education pro-gram. Once these were clear he and they recognized that they wanted to act out their commitment to the church as an ex-tended family in their education program. The congregation implemented a family-cluster education program. Through that program they extended caring ministry to families in crisis in their area. They reached out to single parents, older adults, and others by inviting them to become part of the "extended families" that formed within the nurture program.

The new pastor's relational approach to administration helped the congregation gain positive experiences with change. The new education program showed respect for their values and extended their ministry to others by drawing on their natural gifts. It came into being because the new pastor persisted. He uncovered the source of their resistance and worked with them to develop ministries from within, out of their potential. His relational administration unlocked the resources of this small church. The new ministry was solidly rooted in the potential of the congregation. He did it *with* them, not *in spite of* them.

Relational administrators thrive in small churches because they honor the lifeways of the local culture, because they accept and develop the potential of those with whom they serve, and because they persist.

Questions for Reflection and Discussion

1. Review the characteristics of a relational administrator. Which characteristics fit your style of administration? Which do not? Are there changes you need to make in the way you approach administration?

2. Think about your own work patterns with your congregation. Recall again the characteristics of a relational administrator. Are there changes you want to make in the ways you work with others?

Notes

1. I first included the story of my experience with Mr. Churchill in a paper delivered at the annual meeting of the Religious Research Association in 1976. It then appeared in my chapter in an anthology I edited called *New Possibilities for Small Churches* (New York: The Pilgrim Press, 1983). Reprinted by permission of the publisher, The Pilgrim Press, Cleveland, Ohio.

2. See Sidney Katz, "The Doctor Is Out," *Harrowsmith* No. 46, Vol. VII:4 (December/January 1983), 29-35.

3. "Like an Ever-Flowing Stream: The Rural Church in Maine," Maine Public Broadcasting, Bangor, Maine.

4. Loren B. Mead, *More Than Numbers: The Ways Churches Grow* (Washington, D.C.: The Alban Institute, 1993), 42.

5. Mead, *More Than Numbers*, 60.

6. Mead, *More Than Numbers*, 90.

7. Copies of this videotape can be purchased from Bangor Theological Seminary, 300 Union Street, Bangor, ME 04401.

Chapter 3

How to Do a Lot Well with a Few

During the years I worked as a strategy consultant, I was invited to assess the capability of a very small congregation to reach out to new people who were moving into their parish. Neither the pastor nor the district evangelism committee believed they would respond. The pastor was especially discouraged. He described them as a "stubborn bunch," unwilling to change, and not at all open to new people, especially as leaders. During the interviews I conducted with the thirty-four members of this church a pattern quickly emerged: more than half the people had the same surname. In fact, I discovered that thirty of the thirty-four resident active members were either a "Smith" by blood or by marriage. Late in the afternoon I interviewed the patriarch, J. Catfish Smith. When I asked Mr. Smith whether what I had discovered about the composition of the congregation was accurate, he responded with classic understatement: "Yes, we do have some influence in this church!"

The next day I met with the pastor and district committee to share my findings. When I talked about the dominance of the Smiths, the pastor quickly agreed. "*He's* the problem," the pastor said. "If you want to get anything done, you have to figure out a way to go around him. But that's hard to do because no one will cross him."

Work with, not around, Traditional Leaders

Listening to this leader's analysis I understood why his efforts to introduce changes into the life of that small church were continually frustrated. He could not accept the fact that *any* significant changes in the life of this congregation would be established only with the patriarch's approval. Other pastors who are administrators in small churches experience similar frustrations when they encounter leaders like Mr. Smith. Sherry and I often unlock no small amount of pent-up anger when we lead a workshop for pastor-administrators and include a role play to illustrate the kind of power a traditional leader like Mr. Smith can wield in a small congregation. I usually play him humorously as a Maine "character." At first there is laughter in the group, but it quickly turns to anger during the discussion following the role play. And the anger often increases when it becomes apparent that we are not going to tell those at the workshop how to move patriarchs like Mr. Smith out of the way so that their congregations can "get on with being a church."

In truth, it would be foolish to suggest that an administrator could or should push aside a powerful, traditional leader like Mr. Smith. I found myself bringing this unwelcome news to the district committee gathered to help that thirty-four-member congregation "get on with being a church." Those who establish themselves as effective administrators in small congregations dominated by traditional leaders (and there is at least one of each in nearly every small congregation with which I am familiar) *rarely* try to go around them. If their power is real, one cannot circumvent them successfully—not without great cost.

I am aware that my viewpoint is contrary to the counsel usually offered to those who want to be effective church administrators. The currently popular management-by-objectives approach to church planning at least implies that leaders should be subordinate to objectives. The administrator is advised to guide a congregation's present leaders through a process of strategic planning. Leaders identify and then look critically at their theological assumptions. They study the community that surrounds the congregation to become aware of the needs of those who live in the church's neighborhood and other area concerns the congregation should address. Once the process is complete, they help the congregation develop a mission statement and set goals for the next few years. Church leaders are then committed to implement these goals.

Traditional leaders from the past who frustrate the development of the strategic plan or who stand in the way of changes needed to implement the new goals are characterized as the "old guard." They should be gently but firmly encouraged to step aside. To enable a congregation to make the fundamental changes they need to make to become a "faithful church," it may be necessary to replace old leaders like Mr. Smith with those who represent "new blood."

There are congregations with whom the approach I have just outlined is appropriate. I used it myself on many occasions when I worked as a church strategy consultant with congregations like a new suburban church near the Denver, Colorado, Tech Center. This congregation had grown from 50 to 850 members in four and one-half years! They were struggling to find ways to cope with their dramatic growth. Their three and one-half acre plot of land and recently completed 250-seat sanctuary were already inadequate. Saving seats for visitors each Sunday had become a great challenge. To insure that there would be enough seats for the forty to fifty visitors who usually attended every worship service, church members were asked at the conclusion of each Sunday service to take a red or green tag from jars that contained two hundred of each and hang it along with their name tag on a large board to indicate which service they would attend the following Sunday. During the consultation I moderated heated debates about the size to which the congregation should be permitted to grow. Some leaders believed the church should stay at its present site and accept the limits that location imposed on their growth. A majority argued that the mandates of the gospel required them to relocate to a larger site where they could build a larger building to accommodate those who wanted to join them. Developing a specific mission statement and clear goals were absolutely essential, and very difficult for leaders of this congregation to accomplish.

My years of service as a church strategy consultant taught me that congregations *called* like the Denver church to serve those moving into a growing and changing community need to learn how to develop new programs and include new leaders easily. When I met a seminary classmate at a leadership development conference several years ago, I asked how he had managed to lead his suburban congregation effectively for so many years. "Actually," he replied, "I've been in the same place for sixteen years, but I've served four congregations! The church membership has turned over completely four times while I've been there. Not only that but the character of the membership has changed as well; we have to revise our program and recruit new leaders constantly to keep up with the changes." People whose lives are marked by constant change are served well by congregations like this one that are growing and able to refocus their program and incorporate new leaders.

But methods developed by leaders who serve churches in rapidly changing contexts are not directly transferable to small churches. Those who live in the forefront of change are usually able to benefit from change. They form a subculture that thrives on change. Small congregations are rarely situated in a rapidly changing social context, and when they are, only a few of the highly mobile people from the subculture that thrives on change choose to participate in small congregations. Few small congregations find their social and cultural roots among those who live in the center of social change or who are in a position to manage or benefit from change. Small congregations composed of the original families at a formerly rural crossroads now surrounded by a sea of suburban houses experience those who live in these houses as cultural aliens. Small churches in an inner-city neighborhood composed of members of an ethnic minority and a few remaining representatives of those who used to live in their neighborhood, or small congregations in a rural community that has lost population, are typically made up of people who have not experienced change positively. Many members of these churches do not believe they have the power to manage change to their advantage.

Among those who have experienced change at best as risky, traditional leaders who can resist change play an essential role. They protect the small church and its constituency against potentially harmful changes facilitated by cultural "outsiders" who don't see or appreciate the needs and interests of those who now compose the small church. Even when church members find leaders like Mr. Smith difficult to deal with, they usually still affirm them. He and others like him stand between the congregation and what they perceive as potentially harmful change. They are not likely to shift their allegiance to new leaders until it becomes clear that the changes others want will not be at their expense.

No administrative action can displace traditional leaders in small churches. Displacing them from offices they may hold does not displace them as leaders. Unlike leaders in many midsized and large churches, their power is not based organizationally in the church. It is based beyond the church organization in the social group out of which the church is composed. I sometimes refer to traditional leaders as "contextually rooted" leaders to indicate that their power within the church stems from roots beyond the church. Their authority in the church is derived from the position they hold in the family, community, or ethnic group who composes and often dominates the congregation. So long as their social roots beyond the congregation are solid, attempts to replace or circumvent them within the church are likely to fail.

Unless contextually rooted leaders in a congregation are obviously psychologically dysfunctional, the administrator who wants to succeed in helping a small church become more effective will not try to circumvent or displace them.[1] Traditional leaders hold what Roy Oswald calls "reputational power." In his book *Power Analysis of a Congregation*, Oswald clarifies the critical difference between those who hold formal or official power in a congregation and those who hold informal or unofficial power.[2] An office gives the one who holds it certain rights and privileges and, perhaps, some authority, but not necessarily a lot of power. As the pastor of that thirty-four-member church discovered, there is a difference between what one is authorized to do and what one is able to do. By virtue of his office, the pastor was authorized to lead the congregation but he lacked the power to effect any significant change. The patriarch, on the other hand, held no office; he had no official power. But he controlled everything in the church he wanted to control. The pastor couldn't go around him.

The patriarch held what Roy Oswald calls "reputational power." Traditional leaders who hold reputational power are powerful because others *believe* they are powerful. Participants in small churches expect those who hold reputational power to exercise that power no matter who the official administrator is. I do not mean to imply that traditional leaders *should* be the most powerful leaders in small churches; only that they usually are. An administrator who wishes to become an influential leader in a small congregation must contend with the reality of their power. Effective and even faithful leadership in a small church requires political skill; church administration, like politics, is "the art of the possible." Even Jesus accepted this reality.

After his first sermon, for example, he did not confront the reputational power in the synagogue; he slipped away by merging into the crowd (Luke 4:16-30). He confronted those with reputational power only when his own reputational power was clearly established. Among his own disciples, he did not seek to displace the obstinate and often difficult Peter from his dominant role in the group, but rather worked patiently with him to help him grow in faith and effectiveness.

Working with traditional leaders is usually the best and sometimes the only way to help a small congregation to become more effective and faithful. Several years ago the small congregation where I am a member joined with several others to rehabilitate some substandard housing in our area. When the work was finished, the administrator of the rehabilitation program invited a woman who holds a great deal of reputational power in one of the congregations to become the administrator of the completed housing project. She is a woman in her sixties from an old, established family in the church and community. Little in her past seemed to equip her for this job. Some of us wondered whether she was qualified. We discovered very soon that her reputational power helped her to be qualified. Late one night, shortly after she began working in the new position, the village police called to tell her they were responding to a complaint about a loud party in one of the apartment units. A sizable fight had broken out. She said she would meet the police at the scene of the trouble. When she arrived, the police advised her not to enter the apartment. She ignored their advice and banged loudly on the door to the apartment until someone let her in. She walked into the middle of the brawl and told those involved to stop fighting immediately. They did! She told them to quiet down and sober up. Behavior like theirs this evening would not be tolerated. If they provoked another incident like this one in their apartment, she said she would evict them. They believed her. She has reputational power which, *in the minds* of those fighting, exceeds even that of the police in our village.

With only a minimum of encouragement, those who hold reputational power can play extremely helpful roles in a small congregation. I recall one young pastor in his first year of ministry in a small church who was not at all comfortable when a rather outspoken old attorney was elected to serve as a member of the board in that church. Some members warned the pastor that the attorney had "made trouble" when he served on the board previously. Nearly a year passed before the pastor discovered what kind of "trouble" the attorney would make. The revelation came when the finance committee placed their recommended budget for the coming year before the board. Most items were listed for the same amount as for the current year, including the pastor's travel allowance. He cautiously asked for it to be increased. He had driven more miles than he had expected to drive in the course of his work. Hospitals that serve church members in this rural parish are located in three different directions—all more than forty miles away. How many miles had he driven? the attorney asked rather gruffly. More than twice as many as he had been reimbursed for, and (gathering some courage) he told the board he could substantiate his travel expenses with written evidence! "Well, then, let's see it!" the attorney said. He scrutinized the pastor's records while the board sat in silence. When he was satisfied that the records were accurate, he said, "I don't think the pastor should subsidize the church by paying for his travel expenses out of his salary. I move that the pastor's travel allowance be increased 150 percent!"—and he named the new amount. After a bit of silence, someone seconded the motion. It passed unanimously. After the vote the attorney said, "I will increase my contribution to cover half the cost of the increase."

The secret of becoming an effective administrator in a small congregation lies in discovering which contextually rooted leaders to support. First impressions may be misleading. It often requires patience to discern the true nature of traditional leaders. One pastor who carries administrative responsibility in his small congregation described a member of his board who at first seemed to be simply an obstructionist. A fiscal conservative, he loudly opposed every suggestion that involved more money. One winter day a family of seven who were in desperate straits appeared at the parsonage door. They were entirely out of money. The husband had a job in another city (the pastor verified this fact), but they had no money to buy food and shelter, let alone pay for their travel. Finding them a place to stay for the night exhausted the church's small discretionary fund. At the end of the board meeting that same evening the pastor cautiously shared the family's plight with the board. He braced himself for the outburst he thought was sure to come from the fiscally conservative board member. It was loud, but not in the way he expected. If the pastor was certain these people weren't just "freeloaders," then "we should help them," he said. He would give one hundred dollars, and he prodded the board members to come up with the rest—which they did! When it came to church organizational expenses he was clearly a fiscal conservative. But at the board meeting the pastor-administrator discovered what he wanted to save money for: to enable the church to do "what a church ought to do," namely helping those with real need. This "difficult" leader can be depended on to help persuade others to contribute to local mission. Supporting him will enhance the church's ministries of caring. People give him power not only because he "comes on strong," but because he gives so generously himself. When it comes to ministries of caring, they will follow him.

In thirty years of working with small churches I have found that only a few of those who hold reputational power in small congregations are genuinely disturbed individuals who use their influence in inappropriate or destructive ways. Though there are clearly situations in which the traditional leaders should be challenged to step down, the widespread belief that a new pastor-administrator in a small congregation should move quickly and seek new leaders to bring new life into the congregation is usually not a sound strategy. It feels to them like the administrator is telling the church family to cast out their parents and grandparents who, though they may be difficult at times, are nonetheless worthy of the respect given to them.

Most of those who hold reputational power in a congregation are what I call "caring characters"—potent personalities who have their own, unique way of expressing their care for their church and its ministry. The wise administrator is not put off by them. The fact that most of them do have the welfare of others at heart is the major reason they can maintain their influence—even when they are difficult to get along with. Though they may often say the wrong thing in the wrong way, others respect them because they know their caring is genuine. Discerning which of them to support is often the secret of becoming an effective administrator. In a small church, unlike a large church, there is not an endless supply of potential leaders who could take the places of those currently recognized as leaders. Small churches by nature are not able to include new leaders easily. New leaders, including new pastors, not only must be capable to be accepted; to have real influence they must gain contextually rooted authority. In most small churches members have seen pastors and programs come and go. Strong characters and the leadership they offer may not always be the best, but they persist year after year. An administrator who wants to help a small church become more effective and faithful is most likely to succeed by working with, not by trying to displace or go around, its contextually rooted, traditional leaders.

A Few *Can* Do Well

Several years ago Sherry and I were invited by James Gunn, the staff person in charge of the National Council of Churches' Professional Church Leadership Unit, to study what makes leaders effective in small churches. The research culminated in a national consultation for lay and clergy leaders of small churches. In the final hours of the gathering we suggested that those present divide themselves according to interest into small work groups to prepare a summary of insights. We asked the participants to indicate which group they would like to join by raising their hands as we read a list of possible combinations. Some groups attracted more members than others—which seemed workable to us—until only one person raised his hand when we read the name of a particular group. When I suggested that his would be a *very* small work group, most of the participants laughed.

"No problem," he responded. He was very interested in the topic and would be happy to work alone. For the next two hours the small groups attended to their tasks. In the plenary session that followed, one by one the recorders appointed by each work group shared the insights they identified. When it came his turn (by chance he was the last to report), the man who had worked alone began by noting that his group had little difficulty electing a chairperson and recorder! When the laughter died away, he went on to list the insights he had identified. His suggestions were clear and concise. When he finished reading his list, he thanked the members of his group for their hard work and sat down. The laughter of those gathered turned into sustained applause. His "group" had done the best work of any work group.

I learned something important from that one-person commit-tee, a discovery that has been verified repeatedly in my work with small congregations: It doesn't take a lot of people to complete most of the tasks small congregations face. You can do a lot well with a few. Often, in fact, you can accomplish more with a few than you can with many.

As I recall my own experience with committees in small churches, those constituted of a few people have often been able to do their work more easily and effectively than those made up of many. Sometimes that means only one person. Charlie Dut-ton was the most effective property "committee" I ever worked with. Years of operating his own refrigeration repair business taught him how to get things done and how to get along with people. Charlie was both a skilled administrator and an excel-lent mechanic. He could recognize when a problem was routine and something he could tend to himself, and when it was not and should be brought before the church board or some other group. He was clear, for example, that anything that pertained to the church kitchen or furnishings in the parlor fell within the province of the Women's Guild. He could decide himself about furnace repairs, but the church board would have to be con-sulted when the furnace needed to be replaced. Most of the time Charlie could figure out what was wrong with whatever broke down and either fix it himself or find someone else who could make the needed repair. On many occasions I marveled at his skill (including the day a young boy caused quite a flood when he flushed his sneaker down the church house toilet—Charlie had it out in ten minutes!). I have worked with many property committees over the years; none was more effective than Charlie.

A small congregation functions best organizationally when it is lean and trim. In forming a committee or other work unit, think first about the nature and extent of their responsibilities. Decide what kinds of persons and how many people will be required only when you are clear about the responsibilities they must carry out. Many of the standard organizational plans designed for churches are too complex for small congregations. Make provision only for committees that you actually need; and include only as many members on each as it will require to complete its assigned work. If a committee needs only one or two members to do its work, don't appoint more.

Smaller congregations are especially prone to organizational overweight. Church leaders suffer when they carry excess organization. The leaders of one smaller church complained that there were too few of them to do all of the work that "needed to be done." They were exhausted from the multiple responsibilities each of them carried and worn down by the number of meetings they "had" to attend each month. I sympathized with them, but I told them I thought their overwork was largely unnecessary. They were operating according to an organizational structure that had been defined several decades ago when their church had eight times as many members as it did when we talked. They were exhausted from carrying unnecessary committees with too many members. They found relief by revising their bylaws to specify a much leaner organization.

How a Few Can Do Well

Procedures can make a difference. A small congregation is much more likely to gain maximum benefit from the few leaders who are available when boards and committees follow sound, administrative procedures. Looking back to those years I worked with Charlie, I think he was willing to carry the responsibilities of an entire property committee himself because he hated meetings. He often managed to have a refrigeration unit to repair at the same time the church board met. He would generally arrive halfway through the meeting, in time to give his report. If I am honest with myself, I must admit that many of the meetings I chaired during my early years as an administrator were unnecessarily long. The meetings became shorter and more efficient as I discovered how to help church boards and committees function more effectively. I discovered that:

1. **Appropriate expectations lead to effective meetings.** Those who attend a meeting most often do what they expected to do *before* they come to the meeting. That's why preparing an agenda and sending it out ahead of time is so important. If the agenda is clear, members of a group arrive with a clear understanding of the amount and kind of work they need to do at the meeting. If they know ahead of time that they will face a crowded agenda at the meeting, for example, they are less likely to waste time in the early part of the meeting. If they know in advance that they will be called upon to make difficult deci-

sions, they are able to prepare themselves to make them.

2. **Leaders function best when they understand, accept, and are suited to the kinds of responsibilities they carry.** Learn which roles different leaders in your church *can* play. Some leaders function best as evaluators, others as implementers. I call evaluators "policy people" and implementers "program people." Evaluators are best at analyzing, discussing, and deciding; implementers enjoy designing and doing. Evaluators naturally focus on the process of deciding and, therefore, feel their work is finished when they make a decision. An evaluator who serves on a committee responsible to implement decisions will feel bogged down and frustrated by the details of implementation. An implementer, like Charlie, on a policy board that carefully analyzes and evaluates will complain impatiently that the board talks and talks, but never *does* anything!

Different basic concerns encourage policy people and program people to consider the same proposal from different perspectives. If a new Sunday school curriculum comes before an education committee composed of teachers who will be expected to use it, most of their questions will be practical. How will the children be grouped? Is the material easy to work with? Will we be able to work within the theological orientation of the curriculum? All of these questions anticipate issues teachers expect to face if they are called upon to implement the new curriculum.

If the same curriculum comes before a policy board, their questions will reflect general and normative concerns. Will most members of the congregation be comfortable with the theological orientation of the curriculum? Can the church afford the cost of the material? Are some members likely to object to certain parts of the curriculum, such as a unit on sexuality? These questions are designed to evaluate the proposal's effect on the church as a whole.

Effective administrators understand the different purposes and perspectives of policy boards and program committees and encourage members of each to function appropriately. Expect teachers who serve as a Christian education committee, for example, to be concerned about practical questions that relate to introducing a new curriculum, including details such as the changes in schedule and room arrangement it may call for. Be sure they will have access to specific details at their meeting and plan enough time for a thorough discussion. Don't seek the policy board's approval of a detailed program or other proposal before those who will have to implement it have had time to consider whether they think it is workable. A program committee may justifiably resent being handed a new program they are to implement when they have not had an opportunity to review it and discover whether they can and want to work with it.

Expect members of a policy board to wonder whether a proposal will be too controversial or expensive to justify its approval. Those who want the board to approve a specific proposal or program need to make a case for it. A policy board is more likely to approve a proposal that will cost more or is controversial when they hear the implementers enthusiasm for it and their reasons for wanting to use it. Policy makers who do not have firsthand experience in an area of church life may not be able to appreciate specific concerns connected with implementing programs in that area. And their tendency to focus mostly on those elements of a proposal that might make it more costly or controversial limits their ability to assess whether a new program or other proposal is workable.

In small churches where the same leaders typically carry different responsibilities, often simultaneously, members of a board or program committee are more likely to stray beyond their proper role. When they do take on tasks that are not properly theirs, the administrator can point that out to them. When leaders are functioning as members of the policy board, for example, the administrator reminds them that their job as members of this board is to make general policy. They evaluate and approve programs *as a whole* to be certain that programs and other proposals to be implemented fall within existing policy and budget. If a board begins to plan the details of a program or proposal, the administrator suggests that developing these specifics is the prerogative of those who will have to implement the program. If some board members are also members of the group who will implement the program, the administrator reminds them that they need to do the detailed planning when they meet with the group responsible to implement the program and not at the board meeting.

3. **When introducing something new and substantial, introduce it first as a general proposal, then work out the details.** This order of proceding will help boards and

committees work more effectively. For example, when you discover that the teachers who compose the Christian education committee in your small church are frustrated with the curriculum with which they are now working, encourage them to present the idea of changing curriculums to the church board as a first step. This initial proposal should describe why the teachers are frustrated with the present curriculum and what improvements they seek to gain by adopting a new curriculum. Presenting the proposed shift to the board as a general concept first before they work out the details of the new program is helpful for two reasons. When board members don't have details to consider, they are more likely to give their attention to the policy issues connected with the proposed change. If their first exposure to the idea is in the form of a detailed proposal, they may vote against any change because they object to some minor detail (a particular unit, for example). On the other hand, if the board approves the proposed change in general, they can then refer the matter to an appropriate committee to work out the details. Their referral can list any policy concerns the board may have. This enables the committee to shape a specific program or proposal in the light of these concerns. The final, detailed proposal the committee presents to the board is now likely to be both a program the committee believe they can implement and a proposal that honors the board's policy concerns.

Define Clearly and Evaluate Fairly

During the years I served as a synod executive, I met with a twenty-six-member search committee representing a large church seeking a new senior minister. It took only a few minutes to see that the members of this much-too-large committee were not at all agreed about the duties the new minister should perform. In an effort to resolve their disagreement, I suggested that each member of the committee describe what seemed to him or her to be the *essential* duties the senior minister should perform and how many hours the new minister should devote to each area of responsibility in an average week. As they responded, I listed the suggestions of each committee member according to category and time on a chalkboard, integrating duplicate suggestions. After all members had spoken I summarized their suggestions. Their accumulated list of visions for the new senior pastor included duties in a dozen categories and a typical work week of 156 hours!

When I shared this story with a colleague who serves as pastor of two small churches, he said, "Sounds like my job. Everybody in my churches thinks he or she has the right to define what I should do. There's no way I can please all of them." He went on to explain that some members of the church he serves in a rural lumbering town criticize him for not having more evening Bible study groups, while others fault him for not eating breakfast several mornings each week at the local cafe at 5:30 A.M. with loggers and other woods' workers. Some think he should visit more among the older members; others want him to spend more time on his sermons so that his preaching will be more attractive to the younger adults in the community. His description of the diverse expectations of his congregation goes on and on and on.

A pastor, or any other full- or part-time employee, without the protection of a formal work agreement is vulnerable to the criticism of every church member who chooses to define what the pastor should do. Given the variety of viewpoints that can be present in even a very small congregation, there is no way a pastor who lacks a spelled-out work agreement can please everyone. The pressure from repeated criticism can be disheartening to the pastor and even alienate him or her from those people in a congregation who are offended by the pastor's lack of attention to what they think the minister should be doing.

Both pastors and church boards commonly resist defining a pastor's job. Pastors chafe under the criticism of those whose priorities differ from theirs, yet they resist the thought that anyone has the right to tell them what they should do as ministers. Church boards are reluctant to define the pastor's job because they are hesitant to assume they have the right to tell a clergyperson what he or she should do *as a minister.* They also, perhaps unwittingly, recognize that if they were to define the pastor's job, they, not the pastor, would bear some of the criticism from church members who are not satisfied with what the pastor does. But such a lack of agreement about the pastor's job makes fair criticism and evaluation impossible. How can a congregation determine whether their pastor has done what he or she should do without any prior agreement about the pastor's responsibilities?

I have found that much of the resistance to defining a pastor's job and evaluating a pastor's performance in that job is overcome when pastors and church members distinguish between a pastor's vocation and a pastor's job. It is difficult for others to define or set limits on a pastor's vocation. Vocation for each of us is a personal matter—what we believe God calls us to do. When a pastor says, "I am called to be a minister," he or she is speaking vocationally. We take the statement as a general statement; an indication of the vocation to which this person feels called to give his or her life.

However, when a pastor says, "I am called to be the minister of the North Windham Church," we hear that as a more specific statement. The North Windham Church is a congregation in a particular place with particular issues and needs for leadership. We move naturally to think about what the North Windham Church pastor's work should be. We are ready to discuss the specifics of that pastor's job.

It is helpful both for the pastor and the congregation to be able to distinguish between the pastor's vocation and the pastor's job. When they can make this distinction, the appropriate board or committee can work with the pastor to define areas of responsibility, duties, obligations, and limits they want to include in the pastor's job. They can agree about the number of hours that constitutes a reasonable work week (forty-five *planned* hours is about the maximum that is reasonable). They can specify the areas of responsibility to which the pastor is expected to devote time, and the average number of hours each week the pastor should allocate to various areas. There are at least three advantages to defining a pastor's job in these specific terms.

1. **When what the pastor is to do is spelled out, that information can be made available to every church member.** The pastor and the congregation are then both protected from unfair criticism. Everyone can see where the pastor's *job* begins and where it ends. When both pastor and congregation know what the job consists of, what the pastor is "supposed to do" is no longer simply a matter of opinion. Fair criticism and fair evaluation are more likely to occur. It is possible to measure how well the pastor is fulfilling the terms of his or her agreement. Those who disagree with the way the pastor is spending his or her time can be invited by the pastor, or any other

informed member of the church, to bring their criticism before the appropriate board or committee who can work with the pastor to determine an appropriate response. Serious or repeated criticism may lead the pastor and board to reallocate some of the pastor's time. When the pastor's job is defined publicly, and the procedure for offering criticism of the pastor's performance of that job is also well defined and public, church members are more likely to be responsible when they feel moved to criticize the pastor. I have included an instrument congregations and pastors may use to define and evaluate a pastor's work in Appendix I.

2. **A congregation is much more likely to respond to needs for ministry that the pastor cannot meet when the pastor's job is well defined.** So long as the limits of the pastor's responsibilities are not defined specifically, everyone can easily assume that *the pastor* should be attending to whatever ministry is not being done. But when it is clear that the pastor is working full-time and there is still more ministry to do, the congregation is much more likely to recognize that responding to these additional needs is a *shared* responsibility. Pastor and church leaders can then work together to decide how to respond.

3. **A pastor with a well-defined job is more likely to know when his or her work is finished.** For the pastor's and the church's well-being it is important to distinguish between the pastor's vocation and the pastor's job. While a pastor's vocation is never finished, except for emergencies, when a pastor has worked the number of hours provided for in the agreement with the church board, his or her work is finished. When the day's agenda is full, a pastor has a right to respond to someone with an additional request, "I can't fit that in today; I'll get to it_____." While a pastor can never say, "I am not a minister today," a pastor can say on a day off, "I am not working today; I'll tend to that tomorrow." A clearly defined work agreement enables a pastor to set reasonable boundaries to make space in the midst of a demanding job for leisure and recreation. A clear work agreement protects and enhances a pastor's ministry.

Resolve Tensions before They Lead to Conflict

Conflict can sap the energy of a small church and alienate leaders it can ill afford to lose. Not long after I began to serve as a leader in one small congregation I came upon the lingering effects of a conflict. Others had advised me to "be careful of Doc Smith; he's mad at the church!" Gathering up my courage, I called his home one Saturday afternoon, and when his wife answered the telephone, asked if I might see him. "He's mending fences, but you're welcome to come by. I hope you do. I think it would be good if someone from the church talked with him."

When I arrived he was in the den of the old farmhouse he had rebuilt. After he invited me to have a chair, he asked why I had come. "To find out what happened at that church meeting a year ago and whether there is anything I can do about it," I responded uneasily. For the next hour I heard about what had happened. Before the annual meeting the previous year, the church nominating committee had pleaded with him to let them nominate him to serve on the church board. The only dentist in the area and already "overcommitted" as a volunteer, he had reluctantly agreed. But his acceptance and advocacy for the needs of people who live in the west village, a very poor area, was not popular among some conservatives in the church. After he had agreed to serve, a few church members, "including some of those who pleaded with me to run in the first place," held a "rump" committee session. At the annual church meeting which followed, they nominated one of their number to run against Doc Smith. The other person was elected. "I don't want to work with people who won't shoot straight," he concluded. "Though I see them in town, they won't look straight at me, let alone talk to me when I talk to them."

Doc Smith hadn't participated in the church at all since the meeting. Yet he told me I was the first person who had come to see him in the name of the church since he lost the election. During the years I was a leader and administrator in that congregation, Doc Smith came to worship occasionally—usually on Christmas Eve. He even provided financial support to the church. But the painful rejection he felt at the annual meeting left its mark; he never again served as a leader in that small church.

In retrospect the initial experience that led to Doc Smith's alienation from the church seems relatively minor—the result of covert, evasive tactics on the part of those who were unable to face him directly. Their oblique confrontation with him at the meeting was tense but should not have led to a conflict so serious that it would alienate Doc from the church. Why, then, did it result in a permanent break? I suspect the initial incident turned into a continuing conflict, at least in part, because the congregation lacked well-defined, public procedures members could employ when they found themselves in stressful situations. They didn't know how to prevent the conflict from becoming serious.

During my years of consulting, I discovered countless, similar unnecessary conflicts that alienated valuable leaders and robbed their congregations of the services they might have contributed. Conflict resolution is a complex art that requires insights and skills far beyond the scope of this book.[3] Conflict prevention, by contrast, is much simpler. Taking some simple, straightforward steps to deal with stress when it first occurs is usually sufficient to prevent disagreements from becoming conflicts. If a congregation prescribes and publishes these steps as the way members are to proceed when they disagree, leaders and other church members will be able to resolve most of the stress they encounter before it degenerates into extended conflict. By far the best way to deal with conflict in the church is to prevent it.

To head off destructive conflict I suggest that every congregation define a "grievance" procedure that includes these steps:

1. **Any person who experiences tension with any other person should attempt to resolve that tension** *by dealing directly with that person before pursuing any other strategies.* The responsibility to take the first step toward reconciliation rests with all the parties involved. Whenever conflict is involved, time rarely heals without permanent scars. The message should be clear to every leader and member of the congregation: If you feel aggrieved by someone, or think that someone feels aggrieved by you, *you* are responsible to take the first step toward resolving the tension. And you must talk with the other party(ies) *before* you discuss the grievance with anyone who is not directly involved.

2. **If the attempt to resolve the grievance fails, then ask a mutually agreeable third party for help.** This third party should be someone everyone involved in the disagreement respects, who can bring an unbiased perspective to the disagreement, and who has skills needed to help you resolve the disagreement.

3. **If the third party is not able to help resolve the differences, then all involved should bring the disagreement to a committee constituted and charged to help resolve tensions among church members.** In some polities specified groups already carry this responsibility—for example, the Board of Elders in my denomination, the Reformed Church in America. They are constituted to provide the resources of a caring group, concerned and able to help leaders and members heal rifts before they become serious and continuing conflicts.

This three-step procedure is simple, straightforward, and workable. When church leaders are responsible to hold themselves and others to the steps it prescribes, tensions that are bound to occur within the normal day-to-day life of a congregation will rarely become serious conflicts. Most will be resolved at the level of step one. When a congregation specifies a procedure members are to follow when they disagree or feel aggrieved, they know what steps to take to resolve their disagreements.

A small congregation can ill afford to lose valuable leaders. An effective administrator knows how to help a small church make the most of the few leaders it has and how to help them avoid conflicts that rob the church of leaders who could have given valuable service.

Questions for Reflection and Discussion

1. List the key leaders in your congregation. In what ways does each influence the life and direction of your church(es)? Describe what you need to keep in mind to work effectively with each leader.

2. Are there ways you need to trim down or otherwise change your church organization to make it more efficient?

3. Consider those who hold key leadership responsibilities in your congregation. Which leaders are best at evaluating and which are best at implementing? Are any mismatched in their present positions? If so, how can you help them shift to responsibilities that fit them better?

4. How clearly and realistically are the pastor's and others' responsibilities defined in your congregation(s)?

5. Do you have a well-defined and regular evaluation procedure?

If not, what steps do you need to take to define and implement one?

6. Do you have a well-defined and well-publicized grievance procedure people who participate in your church(es) are expected to follow when they disagree? If not, what steps to you need to take to define and implement one?

Notes

1. Even the most difficult leaders usually fall into the category of characters. A few, however, are genuinely disturbed. For suggestions about dealing with those who are psychologically dysfunctional, see Kenneth C. Haugk, *Antagonists in the Church: How to Identify and Deal with Destructive Conflict* (Minneapolis: Augsburg Publishing House, 1988); Speed B. Leas, *Moving Your Church Through Conflict* (Washington, D.C.: The Alban Institute, 1985), esp. ch. 6.

2. Roy Oswald, *Power Analysis of a Congregation* (Washington, D.C.: The Alban Institute, 1985).

3. Some useful resources are Hugh F. Halverstadt, *Managing Church Conflict* (Louisville, Ky.: Westminister/John Knox, 1991); and Speed B. Leas, *Moving Your Church Through Conflict*.

Chapter 4

How to Do a Lot Well with a Little

It's about one o'clock in the morning when I return home
from my meeting. I am as hungry as I am tired, so I am
delighted to find a piece of pie on the kitchen counter. I sit
down at the kitchen table to eat my pie and try to "unwind"
so I will fall asleep when I go to bed. The house is quiet;
everyone is asleep. I finish eating and decide to sit a little
while to enjoy the silence. But the house is not completely
quiet; something is running somewhere. I follow the sound to
its source, which turns out to be my study. As I reach for the
doorknob, I smell something burning. I open the door very
slowly, relieved that there is no large fire. I almost laugh out
loud at what I discover. The noise is coming from the large,
motor-driven mechanical calculator I used for statistical cal-
culations in those preelectronic days. It has obviously been
running for some time. I can't figure out how to make it stop
running, so I unplug it. I cradle it in an old towel so I won't
burn my hands and set it outside in the yard to cool off.

The next morning when I confront the family at breakfast,
one of my sons—he was about fourteen years old at the time—
confesses. "I set all of the columns to nine and divided by one
just to see how long it would take the machine to calculate the
answer. After it had run for an hour I got tired of waiting for it
to finish and went to bed. I never thought it would catch on fire!"

Only those of us who are at least middle-aged and who grew
up in the old days (defined as "long ago when nobody had a
television" by one of my granddaughters) can fully appreciate
this story. It has taken considerable effort for many of us to learn
to take advantage of electronic calculators and computers.

When they first appeared, these small, noiseless machines seemed mysterious and even ominous to us. When we first heard the term "personal" computer, it seemed a misnomer for a machine that seemed destined to *de*personalize our lives. We or one of our friends had struggled with a mistaken billing or a lost insurance record that took months to correct during those early years when department stores and banks and insurance companies were computerizing.

In the mid-1960s when I returned to school for graduate study, I learned how to use a computer with about the same degree of enthusiasm as I learned statistics. Long after I became computer literate I continued to use my old, familiar typewriter and slide rule—to the despair of my children who insisted I was certain to become a cultural antique if I did not give up these implements of the former age. Eventually I joined the new time completely (I can't remember the last time I used my slide rule). These very words are being typed on a "PC," a personal computer that sits on a table just around the corner from the woodstove in my farmhouse. I was fully converted during my years as a church strategy consultant when I recognized that the PC is not only more efficient and effective, but contrary to my initial expectations, is actually well named. A "personal" computer can help us keep church life personal in the increasingly fast-paced and ever-more-crowded world we now call home.

How to Have an Administrative Assistant and More for $100 a Month or Less

When I first served as a pastor in a small church, I had what every pastor of a small church dreams about: a secretary. Dave Alford and Mel Lynes, two attorneys who served on the church's governing board, contributed some of their secretary's time to the church. For several years I climbed the stairs to their second-floor office each week to give letters, reports, and so forth, to Lorene Pickett to type. She would fit my work in with the work she had to do for them. Lorene's support was a real help to me. She enabled me to spend the hours I would have spent typing on tasks that seem more central to ministry, such as visiting and preparing sermons. And she made me the envy of most of my colleagues who did not have similar help.

Now, three decades later, I am delighted to report that

everyone can have a secretary and administrative assistant who will provide even more help than Lorene gave to me. Every leader who carries administrative responsibilities in a small church can enjoy the excellent personal service of Ms. Dos. Ms. Dos is a true whiz. Ms. Dos will keep your calendar. Ms. Dos will write your letters. Ms. Dos will remember the weekly order of service, take the changes you give her each week, and prepare next Sunday's church bulletin for duplicating. Ms. Dos will prepare a newsletter in attractive format with graphic illustrations and a monthly calendar listing times and places church groups will meet. Ms. Dos will keep all the financial records of your church, analyze them, and prepare understandable and readable reports complete with graphics. Ms. Dos will keep an up-to-date membership list, including information about members' interests, talents, preferences, and whatever else might help you to respond to the personal needs and interests of each. If you are responsible for preaching and leading worship as well as administration, Ms. Dos will keep a file of notes that relate to upcoming sermons, indexed in whatever way is useful to you. Ms. Dos' capabilities are immense—and available at a very modest cost.

MS-DOS is the abbreviation for one of the most popular operating systems utilized by computers. The services that system can provide are available to any church administrator who is willing and able to gain access to a personal computer. If you do not already own or have a PC available to you, I suggest that you do whatever you need to do to buy or gain access to one. *No other single step can add as much to your efficiency as an administrator.*

If you are not already familiar with the world of computers, give yourself some time to discover how a computer can help you become more effective. Look through some of the many magazines designed for those who use personal computers. There are even a few, such as *Church Bytes* and *Christian Computing*, that are designed specifically to meet the needs of church leaders. Spend some time with friends and colleagues who are well acquainted with computers. Pastors and other church leaders who have used computers in their work with the church for some time are probably the best sources of useful information. They have knowledge tempered by experience. The array of data processing options available to church administrators expands almost daily. If you are a beginner (and even after several years of working with computers I still consider myself a beginner), start your own exploration by talking with those who understand what an administrator needs to accomplish in a small church and who have firsthand experience with computer programs designed for church administrators. (In Appendix II there is an analysis of computer software specifically suited to the needs of small congregations. It was prepared by Frank Rogers-Groggett, who began his ministry as a small-church pastor and administrator after working as an industrial manager who implemented computer programs to manage manufacturing operations.)

After only a few conversations you will likely discover that everyone who works with computers has clear preferences. No doubt I have offended a number of readers already by implying that you should employ Ms. Dos rather than Mac. MS-DOS and MAC and the computers that run them (IBM and compatibles and Apple Corporation's Macintosh) are competing operating systems. Each has its advantages and disadvantages—and advocates.

What kind of computer should you have? The answer to that question depends on the tasks you need your computer to perform. Or, to use the jargon of the PC world: choose your software first, then choose the hardware you need to run that software. "Software" refers to programs that equip a computer to perform the functions you want it to carry out. Word processing programs, for example, are designed to support those who work with words; accounting programs support those who work with finances. "Hardware" refers to the computer itself. "Peripherals" are accessories, such as printers, that are attached to the computer.[1]

When you have decided how you want a computer to help you, I recommend that you either encourage your church to purchase its own system or purchase a system yourself. If you are a pastor, ideally you should do both. Then, if you should move to another congregation, you can take your own computer, disk copies of files and other records that are personal with you and leave a fully functioning system for the pastor who succeeds you. Most small congregations will find that less than $2,000 will buy a system that meets all the congregation's and pastor's needs. Used systems can usually be obtained for less than half this amount. Expect to spend $200 to $1,000 a year for maintenance and supplies.

If your means are modest, then buy what you can afford. A system that enables you to do some of what you need to do is better than none. Knowledgeable colleagues and friends can help you set priorities that keep your options open. If you buy the kind of system that is compatible with your needs, you can always upgrade later to a better system when you can afford it. In the past fifteen years I have upgraded several times as I was able to afford improvements. I bought my first system on credit. It was a lot of money and it took me almost two years to pay the debt. But I have never regretted the expenditure. For those of us who must live within limited budgets, the initial investment and maintenance of a computer system is a big expense. But when we consider what the computer helps us do, and what even a part-time secretary would cost by comparison, the expense seems modest.

Word processing, record keeping, and accounting are the three areas in which a computer is likely to be most helpful to church administrators. Writing, correspondence, and record-keeping are all much easier and more personal with the assistance of a suitable word processing program. For example, you can both save time and personalize all your church's correspondence. Anything you want to send to more than one person, or that you will need to send to others at a later time, you need to type only once. Time after time I climbed the stairs to give Lorene a letter of transfer for a church member who had moved away and was joining another congregation. I usually took an old letter, crossed out the names, and wrote in the new names and other corrections. Now I can keep a standard file in my computer called "transfer." When I need to transfer members to another church, I start the program, call up that file, insert the appropriate information and print the letter. I can type in the information quicker than I could correct the copies I used to take to Lorene. And I don't have to take the copy anywhere; I can print it and mail it myself. I can keep a copy of every letter in a file in my computer. If I need to find out when I wrote a letter, I can do so easily and quickly. If the letter is lost, I can run another copy in a flash.

The computer greatly simplifies the weekly task of preparing a Sunday bulletin or printed order of worship. I have files marked "ws1," "ws2," "cs1," "cs2" (abbreviations for "worship service" and "communion service") on my hard drive. Each file contains a different order of worship in outline form. I created these files by typing in the name of each element of the service on a separate line, laid out as I want them to appear in the printed order of worship. For example:

CALL TO WORSHIP
HYMN
PRAYER OF CONFESSION
WORDS OF ASSURANCE

When I want to prepare a specific service of worship, I simply open a new file named "ws," followed by the date of the service. I then copy the appropriate outline file. I work my way through that copied outline file, entering the specific information for the upcoming service. As I choose them, I type in the hymn numbers and titles, Scripture lessons, common prayers, sermon title, and so forth. If I am going to duplicate the bulletin myself, I also enter any information supplied by others, such as special music, print a letter-quality copy and I am ready to make copies for the worshipers. If someone else will supply additional information and print the bulletin, I copy my work onto a floppy disk and take it to whoever needs it. Anyone with a compatible system can insert the disk in that system, add additional information, and print a master copy for duplication. I can repeat the steps easily every time I need to prepare a worship service by inserting the appropriate outline and adding the specifics.

I follow a similar procedure with marriage and funeral services. For example, I keep several marriage services in files on my hard drive. When I visit with a couple who are preparing for marriage, we look through various liturgical options. They can personalize their marriage service by choosing elements from a variety of sources. Using a "split-screen" option in my word processing program I then assemble the service quickly and easily. I place the source file with all the options in the top screen, mark the sections I want to include, and move them to the order of service I am assembling in the bottom screen. When I am finished creating the order of service, I use the "find and replace" option to insert the names of those to be married at the appropriate places in the service. I then print two copies of the service—one in large type for me to read when I conduct the ceremony, and a fancier version to give to the new wife and husband at the end of the ceremony. The entire task takes less than an hour.

An amazing array of support resources literally can be at the fingertips of small-church pastors and administrators. The United Church of Christ, for example, for a modest price offers churches a software library called SAMUEL, an abbreviation for Scripture and Mission—a United Church of Christ Electronic Library. SAMUEL provides monthly resources that include Sunday bulletin themes, lectionary, primary lectionary text, mission moments, offering envelope messages, Sunday bulletin back page messages, and prayer calendar entries for Sundays. Local church leaders who purchase and install this software can access it for their own use. A leader preparing a Sunday bulletin can easily include stewardship messages and prayer calendar entries, even a complete bulletin back page message, from the program material.

The computer greatly expands a church administrator's ability to personalize. Several programs listed in Appendix II include church member records as an option. The user enters basic information for each church member in a data file. Once that file is compiled, an administrator gains much more ability to personalize communication. Suppose, for example, you want to send a notice to the families of all Sunday school children in the congregation inviting them to a picnic at the close of the Sunday school year. In precomputer days I either had to take the notice to Lorene who would type it on to a mimeograph stencil for me, or I had to type it on a stencil myself (with a large bottle of correction fluid handy). Now I begin by calling up the letter I sent last year from the file in which I placed it. I can either make changes to update the letter or write a new one. I then access the file that lists all the names and addresses of church families and create a subfile, or mark electronically, those who have children enrolled in Sunday school. Again I make any needed corrections. I then type the commands that direct my word processing program to write an individual personal letter to every family. It prints a heading, then the name(s) and address of those in each household, an appropriate salutation, the body of the letter I have written, and a signature line. While the computer is printing the letters, I go make myself a cup of coffee. When I return the letters are printed. I type the commands that request the computer to print address labels for the letters it just wrote, insert blank labels in my printer, and press the key that directs it to execute my request. While the printer is printing the labels, I sign the letters, adding a handwritten note to those who seem to me to need a bit of extra encouragement to participate.

In those preelectronic years I wanted to invite everyone personally by sending all of them an individual letter. But I couldn't take the time to write each, and the church couldn't afford a secretary to type all the letters. Now I can easily personalize all church correspondence. When the membership records include information about a member's interests and needs, I can supplement general announcements by sending specific individuals information about events that will interest them. Supported by a computer, small-church leaders can invite personally every young person to a youth retreat, every woman personally to a women's meeting, every man personally to a men's prayer breakfast. The computer helps the small-church administrator and other leaders in the congregation to keep administration relational.

The computer can make administration easier and more personal in nearly every area of church life. A perpetual calendar program can enhance the congregation's ministries of caring. I recall many instances when a church member reminded me to visit another parishioner on a particular day because that was the day the parishioner's loved one had died. With a perpetual calendar program, all that kind of information can be entered and recalled. A pastor and other leaders responsible for ministries of caring can access the perpetual calendar record for the coming week and know immediately whom they should be sure to visit that week. By keeping the calendar up to date, an administrator helps to insure that no one's needs will be overlooked. Birthdays, anniversaries of happy and sad occasions, historical information that is important to the congregation, and whatever else we need to be sure to remember can be entered in the perpetual calendar and will reappear year after year.

Program resources can be purchased to support church leaders responsible for specific programs, such as education and finance. I will discuss assistance a computer can provide in the area of church finance in the next section. In Appendix II Frank

Rogers-Groggett discusses the support several software packages can provide to those responsible for finance in small churches.

An immense variety of software is available to enhance a small congregation's ministry of education, much of it at a surprisingly modest cost. Parsons Technology, for example, offers a program called *QuickVerse* that provides access to eight different English versions of the Bible. Enhancements available include *Nave's Topical Bible*, the *Hebrew and Greek Transliterated Bible* and the *New Scofield Study Bible*. Users can even attach their own study notes directly to Scripture verses.

PC Bible Atlas is a related program available from Parsons Technology. This software includes more than one hundred maps of the Bible. Articles with each map describe locations that appear on the maps. Users can even employ drawing tools included in the program to make their own maps. If you use *PC Bible Atlas* in conjunction with *QuickVerse*, a search feature enables you to find all the places in the Bible where a particular location is mentioned. The search feature also works in the opposite direction. The integrated programs will provide you with a list of all the maps on which any city mentioned in the Bible appears. These Parsons Technology programs are typical of the immense and expanding array of software available to support educational, stewardship, and other program functions.

Administrators and other small-church leaders will also find a variety of resources available in computer networks—systems that link users together by telephone. If you want to access one of these networks, you will need to purchase a modem that permits you to connect your computer to others by telephone. Most networks charge for the time you are connected and, of course, you will have to pay any telephone toll charges, though you can keep costs down by transmitting and receiving during those hours when reduced toll charges are in effect.

Networks offer a wide range of possibilities. For example, ongoing "meetings" are always in progress on general subjects, such as church growth resources, stewardship, and lectionary texts. There are several groups of leaders of small churches who share concerns and insights regularly with one another. Participants in a meeting access the information related to a topic that interests them at a time of their choosing. They can read the information on their computer screens or, if they choose, make printed copies. Participants can respond to the comments of others by adding their own comments to the database.

In 1993, following a growing trend among U. S. denominations, the Southern Baptist Convention initiated *SBCNet*, a data communications network designed for leaders in their congregations and denominational agencies. This information exchange network is available to subscribers through the national communications network, *CompuServe*. *SBCNet* offers participants a wide variety of services, including electronic mail (E-mail) for pastors, resources for ministries, access to SBC publications, teaching aids to supplement SBC Sunday school literature, and conferences.[2] I believe that in the near future, all major denominations will have similar networks linking leaders in their congregations with other church agencies.

When I reflect on the possibilities now available to church leaders through the personal computer and recall how isolated I sometimes felt during my first years as pastor of a rural, small church, I appreciate the special advantages a PC represents for administrators and other leaders in small congregations. Those of us who have a computer and a telephone need never experience the sense of disconnection and isolation I did in those early years. No matter how geographically remote our church may be, we can access the best resources available and communicate easily with others who share our concerns.

How to Take Care of the Church's Money

I recognize the caller's voice when I answer the telephone; he is a good friend who owns a business in the village. "There is something I think I should share with you," he says. "Are you aware that your church treasurer sometimes pays his personal bill at this business with a church check?" I am stunned by the statement. When I recover, I remind him that the treasurer is quite elderly and, perhaps, just becomes confused. I promise to look into the matter immediately. When we finish our conversation, I telephone an attorney who is a church member and tell him I have an urgent matter to discuss with him. He fits me into his schedule and I share the information I have received.

When I finish, the lawyer sits quietly for a moment, and then says, "We will have to confront him." I feel badly about having to do that; the treasurer is an old man who has served the church for many years. But I agree we must get to the bottom of the matter.

We make an appointment with the treasurer. When I tell him what the business owner has told me, he is incensed. "There is obviously some mistake," he says.

"That may be," the attorney responds, "but we will have to have an external audit to protect everyone."

The treasurer objects, but the attorney persists. Suddenly the treasurer is silent. He looks at the floor and then at us. "I'm deeply sorry," he says. "I know that what I have done is wrong; but you must believe me when I say that I planned to replace the money when things got better for me."

Years later when I recall this incident in a conversation with another pastor, he has a different kind of story to share. For three decades the treasurer in his small church offered the church board the same verbal treasurer's report month after month. "The church is solvent," was all he said. The church board knew that to be so, the pastor went on to explain, because all bills were paid each month. "But without a detailed report we never knew exactly how much money came in or exactly how much was spent." Then one day the treasurer had a serious heart attack and died. It took several months to untangle his personal and business finances. In the accounting prepared for the probate court it was clear that the treasurer had regularly transferred funds from his personal account to the church account. The church had actually been operating at a deficit for more than twenty years! The subsidies the treasurer contributed from his own resources were what made the church "solvent" month after month. "His death created a financial crisis," the pastor said. "We discovered we were spending a lot more than we were taking in. We were far from solvent."

Unfortunately these stories are not untypical—especially the second. It is not at all unusual for a treasurer or other financial officer to "rescue" a small church by covering deficits from his or her personal funds. And, sadly, though they are fewer in number, I have discovered more cases than I would like of embezzling by financial officers in small churches.

Small congregations are especially vulnerable to irregular financial practices. Even when they are suspicious, church boards composed mostly of members drawn from one or two extended families, or of neighbors who face each other in many facets of life, hesitate to question or confront treasurers and other financial officers who do not follow proper procedures. Unfortunately this avoidance may perpetuate, even encourage, practices that have sad outcomes for a congregation and those who handle the church's money.

My experience leads me to offer a blunt recommendation to those responsible for administration in small congregations: *Do whatever you need to do to insure that those who handle money in your congregation follow sound accounting procedures.* While you do need to proceed carefully and caringly when you recommend any changes that may be required to institute sound financial practices, be absolutely clear that you will not agree to continue any financial procedures that might put the security of the church's money at risk. When you propose procedural changes, state clearly that you are not questioning the integrity of those currently handling the money. Emphasize the importance of following sound practices, regardless of who is presently entrusted with the care of the church's money. If your church has financial officers who have served for many years, you may want to soften the introduction of your recommendations by suggesting that "times are not now what they once were," or that "we need to make the changes now because you won't always be here to do the job you do." The bottom line: *Do whatever you need to do to protect the limited resources available to your congregation.*

While some administrators may want to seek the advice of a professional accountant, there are three financial procedures that I believe are essential.

1. **Separate income from disbursements.** The person who receives funds and deposits money in the bank and the person who has the power to access those funds to pay bills should *never* be the same person. In the small church where I am a member the person who receives the money, Jean, is called the "collector." Her duties are similar to those of the person who is sometimes called the "financial secretary": she counts the offering, credits individual contributors and deposits contributions received. She then informs Evelyn, the treasurer, of the amount of each deposit. Evelyn is authorized by the session (church board) to pay bills. The ability to receive funds and the ability to disburse funds are separated in different persons. Evelyn cannot receive contributions; Jean cannot withdraw money to

pay bills. That is as it should be.

2. **Regular detailed monthly financial reports and an annual external audit are essential.** If there is no one in the congregation who is familiar with accounting, I suggest that the church board authorize the treasurer to ask an accountant to help him or her set up the church's accounts and reporting procedures. Some of the computer programs discussed in Appendix II include financial management programs. If someone in your congregation can enter the church's financial data within one of these software packages, that program will help to insure that proper accounting procedures are followed. Monthly reports to the board should include at least columns that list figures for:

Budget amount   Current month   Year to date   Last year to date

for both income and expense budgets. Monitoring these figures month by month enables the board to see impending crises before they become serious.

An external audit means an audit by a qualified accountant who is not a member of the church. Engaging and paying a qualified outsider for this service places the audit in the hands of someone who has no direct interest in or access to the accounts he or she is reviewing. That person's approval places all those who have access to the church's money above suspicion. The fact that an audit will occur regularly discourages those who might be tempted to borrow illegally from the church funds. It also helps to prevent the congregation from becoming dependent on well-meaning rescuers who keep the church solvent by subsidizing it with their own funds. Though the benefactor may have the best interests of the church at heart, the sudden loss of his or her subsidy can throw the congregation into a financial crisis they are unprepared to face.

3. **Every expense budget calls for a parallel income budget.** The double-entry principle of accounting requires a stated source for every expenditure. Transferring this principle to budgeting means that a congregation can plan to spend only what they can plan to receive. I find that small congregations project only an expense budget, which everyone refers to as "the" budget. During the early years of my ministry, I recall meeting each fall with the church finance committee to review expenditures during the first ten months of the year. We would

then proceed to draw up a budget for the new year, which was then submitted to the congregation for approval. Often the new budget would total much more than the church could reasonably expect to receive. When the budget was presented at the annual meeting, those who questioned where the "new" money was to come from usually elicited the response "We must have faith" from someone else at the meeting. Unfortunately the doubter's prognosis was generally correct; within a few months the church board was confronted with a stack of unpaid bills and insufficient income. They faced the unhappy task of scaling back the church budget to match the actual income we were receiving.

One way to prevent this unfortunately common pattern is to prepare an income budget. An income budget lists the amounts the congregation can reasonably expect to receive from various sources. It should total the same amount as the other budget that lists what the congregation expects to spend. This other budget is properly termed the "expense" budget.

Preparing an income budget challenges a congregation to consider seriously the sources of its income. Examining and evaluating those sources can help a congregation estimate its income more realistically and anticipate crises that may be in the making. Consider this income budget from Crossroads Baptist Church:

Source	Current	Proposed	Percent
Pledge income	$10,000	$10,000	50.0%
Loose offerings	1,000	1,000	5.0%
Designated gifts	500	500	2.5%
Rent from Day Care	500	500	2.5%
Church organizations	5,000	8,000	40.0%
Total	$17,000	$20,000	100.0%

The board proposes this budget at the annual meeting. They note the total income budgeted for next year is $3,000 more than this year to cover an increase in the pastor's salary and some essential repairs to the building. In the discussion that follows several facts become apparent. The pledge income has been about the same for the past four years. The income from church organizations is largely earned by the women's group at spring and fall public suppers. The largest profit they have realized during the past four years was $4,700—two years ago. Why is the income from church organizations listed at $8,000? A spokesperson for the church board suggests that a third public supper could net $2,500 and increase the women's contribution by that amount. A representative of the women's group objects to his suggestion. She notes that there are fewer and fewer women available each year to work on money-raising projects—that most of the women who put on the public suppers are now in their sixties and seventies; and that the church board has not carried out a stewardship drive for five years. She moves that the budget be amended to increase the amount to be received from pledges by $3,000 and to reduce the amount anticipated from church organizations by $3,000; and that the church board be instructed by the congregation to conduct an every-member canvass during the next month. After some discussion the amendment passes. Listing the sources of income in a budget *to be approved by the congregation* encourages the congregation to examine seriously the amount anticipated from each source and to take steps to be certain the anticipated amounts can be raised.

How to Conserve and Make the Most of Your Congregation's Potential

"That's the third time in as many months we've gotten the same kind of letter!" There is a clear note of annoyance in the board member's voice. "At our August meeting the clerk read a letter inviting our Sunday school teachers to a Sunday school start-up workshop in Boston in September. Remember how we laughed when we read the list of who should attend that workshop? There must have been twenty different kinds of teachers and staff—and us with only five teachers, including Molly who doubles as the superintendent! But the five of us agreed to go. Then in September we got the same kind of letter inviting our "stewardship leaders" to a stewardship workshop, again to be held at a church just outside Boston! Now this month we receive the same kind of letter directed to our worship and music committees inviting worship and music leaders to a workshop in January at another church just outside Boston! Don't the people in those different offices ever talk with one another? Don't they realize that our Sunday school teachers and stewardship leaders and music and worship committee members are all the same people? We're going to be so tired from traveling to meetings in Boston by the winter that we won't care what the next meeting is for!"

"Leader conservation is one of my most important responsibilities," a pastor of two small churches tells me when I share this story with her. "The various mailings we receive inviting us to training and resourcing events assume that we have different leaders to carry out the different program responsibilities in my small churches. Actually the same few people in my churches are responsible for everything. My job (as the church administrator, she might have added) is to help them decide what to take on and what not to try to do. There's no way they can do everything."

Several months ago a new Wal-Mart store opened in Farmington, Maine, about twelve miles from where I live. When the weekly newspaper first announced that this store would be built, local business owners were understandably anxious. How could they expect to compete against this retail giant? Wal-Mart representatives responded to local criticism by conducting a workshop to help small stores in our area learn how they not only could survive but thrive alongside Wal-Mart by offering specific and unique products and services.

In some respects large, "full-service" churches are like Wal-Marts; their strength resides in their ability to offer a full range of program opportunities—something for everyone. Small congregations are more like small businesses; they thrive by concentrating on a few programs and services their individual potential equips them to offer. At the workshop for local business leaders the Wal-Mart representative said, "Don't try to compete directly with Wal-Mart; offer something different."

One might offer similar advice to leaders of small churches. When small congregations try to live according to a large church model, they not only fail to develop their unique potential, they often exhaust their leaders as well. During the years I worked as a consultant, I interviewed hundreds of leaders in all kinds of churches. I always included leaders who had recently resigned or dropped out of their congregations in my samples. I discovered that overwork is the major reason leaders drop out of small churches. A surprising number don't just give up as leaders; they quit the church entirely. Some even start a fight with another church member to provide an excuse for leaving! But the real reason is overwork, which often comes from trying to stretch their church beyond its capability. The most common program development strategies designed for churches today are not suited to small churches. A small church is not like a Wal-Mart; it doesn't have to become larger or meet the varied needs of all those who live in its area or make a profit to fulfill its calling or to survive.

A small church's uniqueness is the most likely source of its strength. Leaders in a small congregation discover their church's unique capability when they concentrate their attention on what they are and can do *as a small church*. An administrator can help a small congregation become aware of *their* potential by asking questions that help them identify that capability. Questions such as, What draws and keeps us together? What do we care about? What are we good at? What are our strengths? What are we capable of offering others? help to clarify that vision.

Several years ago when Paul Ferenczy guided his congregation to develop the unique Christian nurture program I described in chapter 2, these were the kind of questions he encouraged them to ask. The failure of their Sunday school was the crisis that first engaged their attention. But insight came when they stopped focusing on their limits and turned their attention to consider what they *could* do. They discovered that one key strength of their life together stems from their sense of themselves as an extended family. The failure of their old Sunday school program turned out to be a blessing. As they talked with one another about what gives strength to their common life, they recognized that a graded Sunday school that segregates children and adults into small classes according to age is contrary to their basic values. The new style of Christian nurture that brought church members together in homes as extended families to learn and share injected new vitality into their church life and became a means of outreach to their community.

In the years they initiated this program they did little else. They did not seek to enhance their Sunday morning worship, expand their music program, or develop a youth ministry. In other words, they did not feel compelled to become nor feel guilty about not trying to become a full-service church. Both the local pastor who functions as the administrator and denominational staff who worked with this small congregation recognized that developing this nurture program would consume nearly all the creative energy their leaders could muster. Administrators and denominational staff persons who work helpfully with small congregations recognize that they need to concentrate on helping each congregation to discover and accept and develop only their own potential.

When leaders in a small congregation think they have identified their church's potential, the next step is to help them develop that potential. I often suggest a three-step planning model as a helpful way to proceed. I call the model "POST" planning, and diagram it:

Potential

⊢——————→ Objectives ——————→ **ST**rategies

Possibilities

1. **Possibilities**. Determining whether it is really possible to develop the potential we see for our church is an essential reality test. Once we identify what we think may be our potential, we need to test the reality of our assessment. First of all, we need to ask some internal questions. Does the vision we seek to cultivate fulfill our *calling*? Does it express what we believe God wants us to become? Does the potential we seek to develop match our *values*? Does it represent what we really care about? Do we have or can we gather the *resources* required to develop the potential we have identified? Are we equipped or can we become equipped to do what we envision for ourselves as a church?

If these internal questions gain a positive response, then we need to move on to test whether it is possible to fulfill the vision we have of ourselves in the community or area we serve. Is there a need for the ministry we envision? Will some of those who live in the area our church serves respond to the ministry we want to develop?

Several years ago I consulted with leaders of a small congregation who were concerned about the lack of young adults among their members; they told me they needed to develop programs that would attract young adults. I asked them how many unaffiliated young adults were living in their area. They didn't know! We did some research and discovered there were only a few. After looking again at their own resources, they discovered another potential: a capacity to minister to older adults. When community research revealed a slow but steady increase in the number of older adults in their area, they shifted their focus and developed their capacity to minister to older persons. That ministry now challenges and sustains them.

Congregations can maintain efforts that express their calling, that match their values, and that they have the resources to develop. And they are able to translate visions into reality only when some of those who live in the area the church serves respond and benefit from their efforts. A congregation can determine whether it is safe to move ahead to develop the potential they identify by testing whether possibilities within the church and the area support their vision.

2. **Objectives**. When we believe possibilities exist to support the vision we have of our congregation, then the next task is to set specific objectives. Setting a specific objective is the first step in translating an idea into action. An objective is something specific and measurable to be achieved by a particular person or group by a certain date.

"Let's start a new and more relevant nurture program" is an idea. An objective based on the idea is much more specific: Beginning the first week in November the Christian education committee will initiate an extended-family cluster program of worship, education, and fellowship by assembling groups in two homes; each group will bring together fifteen persons representing at least six different households in the church. An objective always specifies what will happen, who will do it, and the date when it will be achieved—what, who, and when. In Appendix I is an instrument designed to help leaders translate ideas into objectives.

3. **STrategies**. The strategies we develop as the final step describe *how* we will achieve our objective. I usually suggest that a group begin planning strategies by making a list of all the tasks that need to be done to implement their objective. Then list the tasks in order of priority: which should be done first, second, and so on. Decide dates that are realistic for the completion of various tasks and who will be responsible to see that each task is carried out. Make a chart that lists each task, who is to do it, and when it is to be completed.

Begin by envisioning your congregation's potential. Then go

on to POST it! Test Whether Possibilities exist to support your vision; write a specific Objective; and spell out STrategies you can follow to implement the objective.

A small congregation that concentrates on developing the potential of one vision at a time will both conserve their resources and maximize their potential. Small congregations *can* develop powerful ministries when they accept their unique potential and are realistic about the possibilities for developing that potential. Small congregations *can* offer unique, vital, and essential ministries. Small churches thrive when they accept and nurture their uniqueness.

Questions for Reflection and Discussion

1. List additional ways a personal computer can enable you to become more effective and efficient as an administrator. Prioritize your list and outline the steps you need to take to implement each suggestion.

2. What, if any, changes do you need to make to take better care of your congregation's money? List steps you can follow to implement each change.

3. Follow the procedure suggestion in the final section of the chapter to identify and develop your congregation's potential.

Notes

1. The descriptions of various components that are included in a personal computer system are for the benefit of those of us who grew up in the pre-PC age.

2. For more information see *Christian Computing*, Vol. 5, No. 12 (December 1993), 20.

Appendix I

Tools for Administrators

This appendix contains sample forms for a pastor's work record and a worksheet for defining objectives. You may photocopy these or design your own.

Following are the areas or categories within which pastors carry on the activities of ministry.

WORSHIP (W): all activities that relate to corporate worship, including time spent planning regular and special services, writing sermons, and time with choirs, and any other activities related to worship.

EDUCATION AND NURTURE (E/N): work with church school, youth groups, confirmation classes, Bible study groups, prayer groups; include all time spent preparing, including meetings with education committees, boards, etc.

ADMINISTRATION (AD): all activity that is concerned with the overall planning and administration of the parish, routine office work, work with committees concerned with personnel, finance, stewardship, property, and buildings.

PASTORAL CARE (PC): general visitation, visiting the sick and bereaved, all activities related to baptism, weddings, funerals.

COUNSELING (CO): all scheduled appointments to counsel those experiencing personal problems, including home visits made for the specific purpose of counseling.

PERSONAL GROWTH (PG): your own prayer and study, alone and with colleagues; continuing education events; support groups.

DENOMINATIONAL AND INTERCHURCH ACTIVITIES (DEN): work with and service in behalf of regional and national church bodies, agencies, and committees; ecumenical activities.

SOCIAL MINISTRY (SOC): working individually or with others to call attention to social issues; working to meet human needs.

EVANGELISM (EV): working individually or with others to share faith with those seeking faith; dialogue with those whose beliefs are different.

OTHER (OTH): all activities not included in the above; in the space provided, describe the activity

Pastor's Daily Work Record for _____(day and date)

Write the abbreviation designated for the category to which you devoted the majority of your time in each half hour. At the end of the day enter the total hours (rounded to the nearest half hour) devoted to that activity.

7:00_____   10:00_____   1:00_____   4:00_____   7:00_____   10:00_____

7:30_____   10:30_____   1:30_____   4:30_____   7:30_____   10:30_____

8:00_____   11:00_____   2:00_____   5:00_____   8:00_____   11:00_____

8:30_____   11:30_____   2:30_____   5:30_____   8:30_____   11:30_____

9:00_____   12:00_____   3:00_____   6:00_____   9:00_____   12:00_____

9:30_____   12:30_____   3:30_____   6:30_____   9:30_____   12:30_____

TOTALS W _____   E/N_____   AD _____   PC _____   CO _____

PG _____   DEN_____   SOC_____   EV _____   OTH_____

Pastor's Work Record Summary for Week Ending _____

Enter the total number of hours you worked in each category for each day of the week.

	Sun	Mon	Tue	Wed	Thu	Fri	Sat	Total
Worship	___	___	___	___	___	___	___	___
Educ./Nur.	___	___	___	___	___	___	___	___
Adminis.	___	___	___	___	___	___	___	___
Past. Care	___	___	___	___	___	___	___	___
Counsel'g	___	___	___	___	___	___	___	___
P. Growth	___	___	___	___	___	___	___	___
Den. Activ	___	___	___	___	___	___	___	___
Social M.	___	___	___	___	___	___	___	___
Evangelism	___	___	___	___	___	___	___	___
Other	___	___	___	___	___	___	___	___
TOTAL	___	___	___	___	___	___	___	___

Pastor's Work Record Summary for Four Weeks

1. Enter the total number of hours you worked in each category during each week.

2. Calculate the percent of work time invested in each category by dividing the total hours in each category by the total number of hours you worked during the entire month.

3. In which categories would you like to invest more or less time? Work with the supervisory committee or board to which you are accountable to decide what changes you would like to make and how you might make them. Agree on a plan of action. Be sure to decide who will carry activities you relinquish.

	W 1	W 2	W 3	W 4	Total	%	More	Less
Worship	___	___	___	___	___	___	___	___
Nurture	___	___	___	___	___	___	___	___
Adminis.	___	___	___	___	___	___	___	___
Past. Care	___	___	___	___	___	___	___	___
Counsel'g	___	___	___	___	___	___	___	___
P. Growth	___	___	___	___	___	___	___	___
Den. Activ.	___	___	___	___	___	___	___	___
Social M.	___	___	___	___	___	___	___	___
Evangelism	___	___	___	___	___	___	___	___
Other	___	___	___	___	___	___	___	___
TOTAL	___	___	___	___	___	___	___	___

Worksheet For Objectives

IDEAS   OBJECTIVES
(Ideas are raw material;   (An objective is a refined idea;
things that might be   it represents something specific
or could happen.)   to be achieved by a certain person or
                               group within a definite period of time.
                               An objective is measurable.)

Develop each idea into at least one objective

Idea	Objective
Idea	Objective
Idea	Objective

Appendix II

Using a Computer in the Small Church

A computer is nothing more than a very sophisticated storage device that remembers and manipulates the information we give it. We can think of the computer as a file cabinet full of empty file folders waiting for information we need to store and use.

We can keep our membership information, including the winter and summer addresses of each parishioner, in our computer. We can monitor church income and expenses with our computer and print reports that compare actual income and expenses with our church budget. We can maintain a yearly calendar that lists the daily schedule of church activities, print the calendar for the current month, and include it in the monthly newsletter. By using a modem, a device that links our computer via telephone to computer networks, we can keep abreast of the latest happening or seminar in our denomination. We can keep our orders of worship in outline form, ready to be filled in and printed for the next service. The computer can use artwork to enhance the readability of the next newsletter. It will entertain our church school children as it teaches them about the Bible. The computer will store the addresses and telephone numbers of all those vendors with whom we deal regularly.

The more familiar we become with our computer, the more ways we discover it can help us. One choir director I know has cataloged the church's sizable music library on her computer. I have seen church school teachers use computer games to teach information that might otherwise be very boring. A computer can connect us to places and people with whom we want to have conversations about such useful topics as youth groups, fund raising, worship resources, even a discussion about this week's upcoming sermon. In short, the computer is a gateway to information and resources that can make ministry easier and more effective.

Most people use the word "computer" as a collective term to describe several interconnected components. *Hardware* includes the computer itself and the keyboard, printer, and screen—anything that attaches to the computer and assists it in its work. *Input devices*, as the name implies, include such components as the keyboard, disks (including floppy, hard, and CD's [compact disks]), scanners, and modems that bring information into the computer. *Output devices*, such as a printer, speaker, or disk, transmit information out of the computer. *Size* refers to the amount of storage space a computer has. A minimum of 120 MB (MB = mega bytes = 1000 bytes) of space in a hard drive is essential if you want to take advantage of many of the programs available today. That minimum is likely to change upward as software programs become more intelligent. The *speed* of a computer is measured by HZ, which stands for hertz. The higher the number, the faster the machine. Speed makes the most difference when we ask our computer to perform complex tasks or to work through a lot of information, like sorting information from our database of church members or printing something that contains a lot of pictures. More *onboard memory* (RAM = random access memory) also enables a computer to work faster—if the program we are using is written to take advantage of it.

A printer attached to our computer enables us to print information the computer processes. Dot-matrix printers are the least expensive printers available today. Bubble-jet printers are more expensive but produce a printed product with better quality. Laser printers are fastest and produce the best-quality printed product. I prefer the quietness, quality, and speed of the laser printer, especially when it comes to producing professional-looking documents. Hewlett Packard has set the standards in the laser and bubble-jet printer markets, as has Epson in the dot-matrix market. These are quality, proven manufacturers.

When it is time to shop for a computer, we need to know not

only what we want our computer to accomplish but also how much money we have to spend. The newest computer is usually the most expensive and fastest model available. As businesses upgrade to take advantage of new technology, older models become available, at a considerably reduced price, through repair centers and mail-order advertisements. The size of the church and the type and quantity of information we need to record and manipulate dictate how large and powerful a computer we need. Most programs will specify what capacities are required for them to perform well. If they don't, don't buy them.

The *software program* is the mind that drives the computer. Each program enables us to organize and manipulate information in the ways that serve our needs. A surprising number of software programs have been written to meet the particular needs of small congregations. At the end of this appendix I have listed and compared a few that are currently available. It is important not to compromise when choosing software. Purchase a program only when you are certain that it has the ability to meet your needs. For example, if your membership role includes a lot of people who have multiple addresses, find a program that can handle multiple addresses.

Sometimes church members who work with computers will offer to write a program for the church's use. Personally, I find a gracious way to refuse their help. I have found that these volunteers are less willing to help as time passes and may not be available when we need them to clarify instructions or to help us with some unanticipated difficulty with their program. I have found it better to seek their help when I am choosing which hardware or software to buy. With rare exception the software needed is already available—with help readily accessible by calling an 800 number.

Word-processing programs are essential for many of the tasks administrators and other leaders are called upon to perform in small churches. The two most popular programs are published by WordPerfect and Microsoft. These are powerful programs that contain features to help with weekly tasks, such as writing letters and sermons, and with more complex tasks, such as formatting material in booklet style to print by-laws, directories, or worship bulletins. I find it helpful to have a word-processing program that will import information from other sources. With this import function as an integral part of my word-processing program, I can edit what I receive from others. I need to print only the relevant parts of an imported document. Many major software companies like WordPerfect and Microsoft have a marketing policy to sell their programs to nonprofit organizations at a discount. Specific information can be obtained by calling their toll-free number, which is obtainable from the 800 operator (1-800-555-1212).

One important factor to consider in selecting a program is how long it will take to learn to use the program. Complex and poorly written programs may not be "user friendly" and may be difficult to learn to use. I must confess that I often believe I can run a program without looking carefully at the instructions. I usually discover, perhaps weeks or months later, that there are features I didn't know about that would have saved me lots of time if I had carefully taken the time to learn to use the program in the first place. Some programs are complicated enough that there are user groups that meet to offer help to one another and to share what the software has accomplished for them.

Some of the programs suggested for use in small churches come in modules that various church leaders can install on their own computers at home. These programs will also integrate the information among modules when the modules are installed in a single computer. Typical modules may include membership, attendance, contributions, and finance. A membership module, for example, tracks addresses, phone numbers, titles, gender, functional dates, envelope numbers, and group information. From this information address labels, directories, or other reports can be generated that are configured to our needs. Notes about special needs or visitation may be included as a part of the software. The attendance feature included in some membership modules can analyze which church members are present at worship services and other meetings. I have found in my work with small congregations that this feature is not necessarily helpful. There are so few of us that we all know who is missing! A spreadsheet module (or program) records and manipulates financial information. We can then plot that information on graphs and *see* how much has been given per member or what percentage of the total budget is allocated to missions or fuel costs or staff salaries, and so on.

A finance module that makes financial information easily

accessible to the leadership of the church can be very helpful. It can enable us to record contributions to various funds and print statements that are not only necessary for income tax purposes but also provide parishioners with a quarterly summary of their contributions. A finance module can help us plan church budgets and then track income and expenses related to each budget on a weekly or monthly basis. Financial modules are very helpful if we need to manage several funds.

Gaining up-to-date information about software packages and hardware can help you keep abreast of innovations that may be helpful to you. A number of magazines are available, many of them aimed at users of specific types of hardware and software. You may find them at local stores or at community or college libraries. One of the most popular and usable publications is *Computer Shopper.* This is a monthly publication that reviews new software and hardware and contains hundreds of suppliers who are competing for your business. *Church Bytes* and *Christian Computing* are designed specifically to meet the needs of church users.

What follows is a brief review of a few IBM-compatible software programs that are useful for the small church. Many more programs have been written, and this list is offered as an indication of the price range and possibility of these tools. Unless otherwise indicated, these programs deal with the entry and manipulation of membership data, contributions data, fund balances, and checkbook activity. Be aware that the larger and more powerful the program, the more information it requires to complete the work we ask of it and therefore will require more of our time. In the small church there is a point at which the computer can become a burden rather than a tool, and one should be ever cautious of that slippery slope.

Some Resources

Christian Computing Magazine
P.O. Box 198
Raymore, MO 64083
(816) 331-3881

Church Bytes, Inc.
562 Brightleaf Sq. #9
905 West Main St.
Durham, NC 27701
(919) 490-8927
Magazine subscription is $18.00 per year for 8 issues. Helpful to all areas of church administration and leadership in the area of computer use. Publishes extensive reviews of software programs for PC and Mac hardware.

ECUNET
800 RE-ECUNET/ (800) 733-2863
A telecommunication network that includes many denominations. Discussion about timely topics that impact our culture and the church.

PARSONS TECHNOLOGY : *Membership Plus, Money Counts*

Space - RAM	512K
Hard Drive	4-5 MB; can be run on dual-floppy drives
Membership	yes
Households	0
Demo Disk	no, 30-day trial
Groups/activities	yes
Member Status	yes
Attendance	yes
Contributions	yes
Financial Package	*Money Counts*
Sort on Specific Field	yes
Mail Lists	yes
Export Data	yes
Cost of Program	2 Programs $99
Support by Supplier	Phone or Computer BBS

Parsons Technology is a software provider of many church-related software programs. The *Membership Plus* program can be purchased with the accounting program, *Money Counts,* at a discount. *Membership Plus* deals with the membership, attendance, and contributions functions, and *Money Counts* is a financial program that keeps track of your income, expenses, checkbook, and any asset holding, such as endowments, trust, and special funds, as well as tracking the budget. They can be used together, transferring information such as the total contributions to the checkbook. The two programs also share information about the fund balances.

This is the least expensive program that provides the basic information for keeping records on the congregation. The import function allows member information to be imported into a word processor to be merged with a letter or sorted for other uses and communications. Do not be deceived by the low price. We have consulted with people who had not read the manual and did not receive the full capabilities from this program.

This program will work without a hard drive; however, Parsons does not recommend that practice since the speed will be much slower.

Access to no-charge technical information is accomplished through a phone number or through the on-line service of CompuServe and GENIE. **Contact**: Parsons Technology, One Parsons Drive, P.O. Box 100, Hiawatha, IA 52233-0100. (800) 223-6925/(319) 395-7300

CONCORDIA COMPUTER SOFTWARE : *Ministry Information System*

Space - RAM	640K
Hard Drive	7-10MB
Membership	500
Households	250
Demo Disk	yes
Groups/activities	yes
Member Status	yes
Attendance	yes
Financial Package	*Single Fund, Check Book*
Contributions	yes
Sort on Specific Field	yes
Mail Lists	yes
Export Data	WordStar, WordPerfect
Cost of Program	M,C,C, for all 3 $495 or $199 ea
Support by Supplier	yes

Concordia has an assortment of administrative programs that are written for the small, midsize, and large church as well as Bible-based game software. This program is specifically for the small church. The $495 price includes Membership, Contributions, and Checkbook modules, or they can be purchased separately for $199 each. Users of a smaller system can upgrade and transfer their information to a larger system by purchasing the larger system.

This software supplier indicates that over 3,500 systems have been purchased. Each module can be used on a separate computer or share the same computer and therefore share information. This is helpful for those people who would rather work in their own home or for churches who do not own a computer. A ninety-day guarantee is offered. **Contact**: Concordia Publishing House, Computer Products Department, 3558 South Jefferson Ave., St. Louis, MO 63118-9968, (800) 325-2399

OMEGA C.G. LIMITED : *Alpha System*

Space - RAM	640K
Hard Drive	7-20 MB
Membership	yes
Households	yes
Demo Disk	yes
Groups/activities	yes
Member Status	yes
Attendance	yes
Financial Package	*General Ledger +*
Contributions	yes
Sort on Specific Field	yes
Mail Lists	yes
Export Data	yes
Cost of Program	$495
Support by Supplier	$200 yr

The *Alpha System* is for small churches. It is a flexible program that allows a certain amount of customizing of the information.

The reports can be customized with a special header or footer of your choice. In the financial area, the reports yield percentage, which is a helpful tool for comparison to the whole congregation.

Directories are a normal feature of these programs with the added feature here of printing geographic codes or placing neighborhoods together in the directory.

The printed statement of contributions is very clear and nonthreatening when the givers receive the notice of where their contributions have been posted and what remains as a balance on their pledge.

There are five levels of security so that the information the church has collected remains confidential. This also insures that information is not changed by one individual.

There is a hot-line that is used for assistance if you are not able to figure out a report or a function with the supplied manuals. There is an additional cost after the first thirty days for using the hot-line. **Contact**: Omega C. G. Limited, 377 East Butterfield Road, Suite 675, Lombard, IL 60148. (800) 443-3481/(312) 969-7799

AUTOMATED CHURCH SYSTEM : *Automated Church System ACS*

Space - RAM	640K
Hard Drive	40MB recommended
Membership	unlimited
Households	300
Demo Disk	yes
Groups/activities	yes
Member Status	yes
Attendance	possibly extra $
Financial Package	possibly extra $
Contributions	yes
Sort on Specific Field	yes
Mail Lists	yes
Export Data	yes
Cost of Program	NA
Support by Supplier	NA

This is a very flexible system that has the ability to customize the screens your church will use most. There are custom printed forms available for your church.

The program called the ACS 2-PLUS-1 sells for $595, which includes Membership and Contribution modules and can include one of fourteen other modules (attendance, visitation/prospects, special mailing, general ledger, payroll, accounts payable, purchase order, accounts receivable, calendar/facility scheduling, reservations, music library, media library, assets inventory, report generator, and denominational reports). The entire package costs $4,875 and a five-module package costs $1,875.

There is a voice message system that can be used with this package that will automatically place a phone call to a specific group of members and leave a recorded message with them.

Training sessions are available at your location or at another training site. Support is charged at $2 per minute, as required, or up to $89 per month for unlimited support through an 800 number.

Computer-generated photographs of members may also be accessed in that member's field. **Contact**: Automated Church Systems, P.O. Box 3990, Florence, South Carolina 29501. (800) 736-7425/(803) 662-1681

THE SOFTWARE LIBRARY : *Church Management Systems*

Space - RAM	512K
Hard Drive	2-3 MB, per module
Membership	separate module
Households	yes
Demo Disk	yes
Groups/activities	yes
Member Status	yes
Attendance	separate module
Financial Package	separate module
Contributions	separate module
Sort on Specific Field	yes
Mail Lists	yes
Export Data	yes
Cost of Program	$295-$795
Support by Supplier	varies

CMS is sold in modules. Membership, Contribution, and Finance are about $795 for each module. Attendance is $395 and Payroll is $495. Multi-user network versions cost more. There is special pricing for the small church, which may bring the cost down to $295 for each module. Training seminars are available at a cost as are annual support agreements. The Software Library offers time payment plans as well.

This program has the standard features and an expanded report formatting feature. If the reports available are not sufficient, the export feature will allow different reports to be formatted with a word processor. **Contact**: The Software Library, 330 Bass Lake Road, Suite 304, Brooklyn Center, MN 55429. (800) 247-8044/ (612) 566-4212

Other Titles in the Small Church in Action Series

Christian Education in the Small Church

Donald L. Griggs, Judy McKay Walther. Quality programs on a tight budget are the goal of a holistic approach to education covering all ages and all church activities. Filled with new ideas for tailoring programs to community needs, designing a curriculum, selecting the resources, building relationships between education and worship, equipping leaders, and much more.

0-8170-1103-X

Developing Your Small Church's Potential

Carl S. Dudley, Douglas Alan Walrath. Dynamic possibilities for churches struggling to survive despite dwindling memberships. New ideas for making positive use of community transition, absorbing newcomers into the church family, reshaping the church's image, and developing programs reflecting community needs. 0-8170-1120-X

Activating Leadership in the Small Church

Steve Burt. People-oriented ideas for encouraging members to volunteer, relational skills needed by pastor and leaders, procedures for selecting a pastor, and twelve helpful guidelines for assessing small-church ministry, mission, and programming. 0-8170-1099-8

Money, Motivation, and Mission in the Small Church

Anthony Pappas. An on-the-job understanding of the small-church culture, what motivates members, and fund-raising ideas. Shows pastors and lay leaders how to develop big-impact mission projects with limited resources, provide pastors with fair compensation, tap new sources of funds for building maintenance, plan realistic budgets, and much more.

0-8170-1146-3

Mission: The Small Church Reaches Out

Anthony Pappas, Scott Planting. Will convince you that small churches can be strong and vital in mission outreach. Emphasizes prayer as the starting point for determining your own church's mission and offers specific ideas to guide you through the process of revitalizing or building a mission outreach that makes a real difference in the lives of the people it touches.

0-8170-1174-9

Caring for the Small Church: Insights from Women in Ministry

Nancy T. Foltz. Men and women frequently use different skills in solving problems. Although the challenges awaiting ministers of small churches are not gender-specific, gender can often make a difference between success and frustration. Highlights areas where the natural gifts of womanhood nurture small-church ministries and vice versa.   0-8170-1175-7